Angel Therapy

Also by Doreen Virtue, Ph.D.

All of the above are available at your local bookstore, or may be ordered by visiting: Hay House UK: **www.hayhouse.co.uk** • Hay House USA: **www.hayhouse.com;** Hay House Australia: **www.hayhouse.com.au;** • Hay House South Africa: **www.hayhouse.co.za**

Doreen's Website: **www.AngelTherapy.com**

❤ ❤ ❤

Angel Therapy

Healing Messages for Every Area of Your Life

Doreen Virtue, Ph.D.,

and The Angelic Realm

HAY HOUSE

Australia • Canada • Hong Kong
South Africa • United Kingdom • United States

First published and distributed in the United Kingdom by Hay House UK Ltd, 292B Kensal Rd, London W10 5BE. Tel.: (44) 20 8962 1230; Fax: (44) 20 8962 1239. www.hayhouse.co.uk

Published and distributed in the United States of America by Hay House, Inc., PO Box 5100, Carlsbad, CA 92018-5100. Tel.: (1) 760 431 7695 or (800) 654 5126; Fax (1) 760 431 6948 or (800) 650 5115. www.hayhouse.com

Published and distributed in Australia by Hay House Australia Ltd, 18/36 Ralph St, Alexandra NSW 2015. Tel.: (61) 2 9669 4299; Fax: (61) 2 9669 4144. www.hayhouse.com.au

Published and distributed in the Republic of South Africa by Hay House SA (Pty), Ltd, PO Box 990, Witkoppen 2068. Tel./Fax: (27) 11 467 8904. www.hayhouse.co.za

Distributed in Canada by Raincoast, 9050 Shaughnessy St, Vancouver, BC V6P 6E5. Tel.: (1) 604 323 7100; Fax: (1) 604 323 2600

The author of this book does not dispense medical advice or prescribe the use of any technique as a form of treatment for physical or medical problems without the advice of a physician, either directly or indirectly. The intent of the author is only to offer information of a general nature to help you in your quest for emotional and spiritual well-being. In the event you use any of the information in this book for yourself, which is your constitutional right, the author and the publisher assume no responsibility for your actions.

A catalogue record for this book is available from the British Library.

ISBN 978-1-4019-1050-5

Printed and bound in Great Britain by TJ International Ltd, Padstow, Cornwall.

To Pearl and Frederique
— Doreen Virtue

♥ ♥ ♥

To you who are the
infinite light of the universe
— The Angels

Contents

PART I: The Healing Messages

PART II: Communicating, Healing, and Living with Angels

Preface from Doreen Virtue, Ph.D.

Late at night, as a little girl, a strong and loving force would sometimes awaken me suddenly. In my darkened room, I'd see sparkling lights and feel surrounded by an unearthly love that let me know my angels were near. Then, I'd fall back into a sound sleep, assured that I was safe and protected by great, gentle beings.

Over the years, as I pursued my doctoral degree, got married, and had children, I lost contact with the angels. While I still loved everything about them, I stopped talking to them. Occasionally, I'd hear a spiritual voice directing me to make changes in my life. Yet, because my life was so hectic and busy, I often ignored the wisdom of my angel's guidance.

That all changed on July 15, 1995, as I was dressing for an appointment I had at a church in Anaheim, California. An angel's voice outside and above my right ear said, "Doreen, you'd better put the top up on your car, or it will get stolen." I was in a big hurry, so I considered the voice as more of an irritant than a help.

I don't have an extra five minutes to put up my car top! I thought. My white convertible car is ordinary looking when its black cloth top is up, but with its top down, the car is a bit showy. Clearly, the angel wanted me to be unobtrusive so as not to attract the attention of a car thief. The voice continued its warnings about car thieves, but I stubbornly insisted that I had no time to spare.

On the way to my appointment, I felt a negative energy surround my car like a thick fog. Something told me, "Someone has just spotted my car with intentions of stealing it." I was certain that someone would steal my car, so I prayed for protection as I pulled into the church parking lot for my appointment. I parked close to the church, and as I got out of my car, a male voice behind me screamed at me to give him my car keys and purse. My angel's warning had been accurate!

I followed an inner directive that told me to scream with all my might. My shrieks caught the attention of a woman sitting in her car across the parking lot, and she leaned on her horn. All the noise caused the people inside the church to come outside, and the car thief and his accomplice ran away. I was unharmed, and I still had my purse and car. When I called the police to report the crime, I learned that the car thieves, armed with a gun and a knife, had been on a crime spree that day.

That was the day I learned my lesson about listening to my angels! Not only did I begin listening to angels, but I also actively solicited their guidance and help. The more time I spent conversing with angels, the more easily I could hear their loving wisdom.

In my therapy sessions, I began helping my clients hear their own angels. Today, I often act as an intermediary who delivers messages to my clients from their angels. The healing power of the angels exceeds any form of "man-made" therapy I have ever witnessed. The angels have wonderful gifts from God to impart to us. So, I am excited that many of us desire to connect with these divine messengers.

The angels have a different way of seeing ordinary situations. Their messages help us heal our beliefs and thoughts by offering us empowering, loving viewpoints. They teach us how to use our spiritual senses to see, hear, feel, and know the real world that transcends the illusory world's problems.

The angels' style of speaking and vocabulary often seems different from our own. This is partly, I think, because they see the world differently than we ordinarily do. They view everything with love and compassion, and their priorities can differ from our own. Since angels have full use of their spiritual senses, they can see, feel, know, and hear things beyond the physical world. These are some of the reasons why the angelic messages in Part I of this book may, at first glance, seem difficult to read. However, if you spend time reading and meditating upon the words, I think you will soon become accustomed to the angels' unique cadence and point of view. Allow yourself to be swept away by their beautiful perspective, and you'll find the healing power in the center of their messages.

The angels really do offer a great deal of practical wisdom, which we can immediately put into practice. They teach us ways to heal our relationships, our careers, and our health. Seemingly, no problem is too small or embarrassing for the angels. Their message to us is clear: *"Give everything to us, and we will give it to the light of God, where Love purifies all seeming problems."*

In this book, I hope to fully immerse you in the healing energy of angels on earth and in heaven. This book has two parts: In Part I, the angels channeled the entire text. After praying for their guidance, I would lose consciousness of my body while The Angelic Realm transcribed through my mind and hands directly onto the keyboard of my computer. Often, I would hear their words as they would enter my hands and become typewritten on the screen. Other times, the words completely bypassed my conscious awareness and directly became written sentences on the computer screen.

Rarely was I aware of what the angels were writing through me. In fact, at times, I firmly believed I was typing gibberish. I would set the writing aside, fully expecting that I would see meaningless letters instead of coherent words and sentences. Then, when I'd later read the channeled material, the angels' profound and sweet messages deeply moved me. I learned a great deal from these angelic messages!

I knew the angel channeling was not of my own making for several reasons. First, many ideas and viewpoints that came through were entirely original to me and did not reflect any reading, learning, or introspection I recall personally undertaking.

Second, the vocabulary and syntax choices were different from my own. Often, the angels chose words that were foreign to me. Or, they dictated words that did not make sense. At these times, I'd ask them, "Are you sure this is the word you want me to write?" They would then either give me the go-ahead or correct my understanding of their intended words. For instance, once I wrote the word *ring,* when they had actually channeled the word *sing.* I also checked the angels' unfamiliar words in my unabridged dictionary. Invariably, I'd find that their grammar and word usage was not only correct, but also reflected deliberate choices to convey specific meanings.

Sometimes, as I'd reread the angel channelings, I'd find that it wasn't any specific word or phrase that moved me; it was the overall tone of the passage. The angelic energy has a soft, velvety feel to it. If you measured it on an oscilloscope, its vibration would undoubtedly top the charts in high-frequency ranges.

Jill Kramer, the editorial director of Hay House, and I have left the messages intact (largely unedited), so you will read the words exactly as the angels delivered them through me. The only editing to the original messages consists of adding punctuation, breaking up run-on sentences and paragraphs, and making spelling corrections. Occasionally, I decided to eliminate redundant or ambiguous sentences from the messages. I also reworded some phrases that were unclear because of archaic vocabulary. For example, I changed "Think not . . ." to "Do not think. . . ." Along the same lines, I deleted some words and phrases, which, to me, made sentences difficult to read; for instance, I changed "at this very time" to "at this time." I made these changes only after the angels communicated their approval, and when rewording led to greater clarity without losing the message's meaning. At other times, when I asked the angels to reword the sentences in a more modern way, they readily helped. The angels also asked me to leave in some sentences that confused me, assuring me that in time, these messages would make sense.

When I first channeled The Angelic Realm, I couldn't withstand their high frequency for long periods. After about 15 minutes of channeling, my head would feel numb. Like rich chocolatey fudge, the angels' energy was too rich, too sweet to consume more than a little morsel at a time. Gradually—through the steps described in Part II of this book—my own frequency was cleared and raised so that I could channel for longer periods.

The angelic messages vibrate at such a high level that you may find it difficult to digest more than a few pages at a sitting. Partially, this difficulty comes from our lower-self egos, which do not want us to communicate with the angels. The ego knows that if we fully listen to God and the angels, fear will be eliminated. And the ego's whole life force is fear. So, your ego may try to dissuade you from angel communications. Some of the ego's "tricks" include having you get sleepy, hungry, thirsty, or distracted as you read the angels' messages or attempt to communicate with them.

The angels have presented comforting, healing messages about various human conditions such as fear, addictions, and finances. You may want to read specific pages related to a current situation in your life. It's also helpful to simply flip through the book and read the page that opens naturally for you. Notice how perfectly this page fits your current questions and desires.

In their messages, the angels don't always suggest specific things to "do" to feel better. The healing in their messages is on a deeper level, where it triggers changes in our outlook or decisions to rid ourselves of painful beliefs. The angels' words emanate from love, and so just reading the messages elevates our thoughts and feelings from fear frequencies to love frequencies. We vibrate at the angelic level as we allow our thoughts to ascend and soar to their heavenly energy rate.

In Part II of this book, we have offered specific guidance on ways to create closer relationships and communication with the spiritual realm. Whether you desire to talk to angels, God, Jesus, some other spiritual being, or your dearly departed loved ones, you certainly have all the tools available for divine communication.

The angels have asked me to emphasize that their communication in this book is but one of many steps in a healing path of spiritual growth. Use their words to open a portal of light in any area of your life where darkness seems to reign. Then ask the angels to help you to widen this beam of light until it fills your entire consciousness and permeates your life.

♥ ♥ ♥

Preface from
The Angelic Realm

You are indeed an earthly angel sent here by God to per-form miraculous deeds of love and sharing. You are beloved and loving, and we heavenly angels are here to support and guide you. We will help you to purify your life and life vessel to bring you in harmony with the infinite symphony of earthly music that you can share.

This book is a vehicle of our sharings to you who desire to raise your internal vibrations so that more and more light can enter your sphere. We know that you suffer at times need-lessly, because you believe you are alone and friendless. Let us assure you that you are not! We are always available for guidance and comfort and will shine the light of love upon any problem with which you wrestle. Let us share your pain, and we will shine it away.

Each of you is different, yet in so many ways you are ex-actly alike. In the pages of this book, we have guided Dr. Doreen Virtue's hands and mind to share with you some of our thoughts about earthly problems common to you all. We also want you to know that we are available for individual consultation as needed. So when you are alone and blue, reach up and above you. There is always an angel in the room with you, an angel who—if not able to bring the whole of heaven into your consciousness—can at least settle the score in your own mind and heart so that you may be at peace.

Pull down the shades on sorrow, and flip through the pages of this book whenever you feel lonely or depressed, or in need of inspiration. Each topic is in alphabetical order, so you can look at the Contents section to see which inspiring note would be a blessing to you that day.

Might we also suggest that you allow your mind to wander and simply open the book to a page. Trust that your guidance will allow you to find the page that will best impress upon your mind for this day. The radiation of your vibration will magnetically draw you to just the right words for settling your score.

As you read, have faith about what you hear within. For your own angels will sing in harmony with our words in this book. The beauty of your own internal choir is cause for you to rejoice, if you will stay with it in stillness with yourself as you read our words within this book.

Our greatest joy is lighting the candle flame of God's love within your heart, causing you to thirst and hunger for even greater joy. This drive for love, we know, will draw you away from earthly concerns and will put you on the well-worn path of golden light leading straight to heaven. This path within you awaits your desire right now, and we are here, always patient and glad to assist you whenever you feel unsure of your foothold. Just one thought, one cry for our help, and we are there with you.

We are here with you always, beloved. We ask that you enfold us in your heart wings, and cry upon our shoulders until the tears flow no more. You are home with us here, and you have never left our side. You are truly a thing of beauty to behold, and we wash away your tears of sorrow with reminders that there is nothing to do but rejoice, because God made you always and forever our brother and sister in cause.

♥ ♥ ♥

Acknowledgements

God, the angels, and some very angelic people all worked together to create this book. Eternal gratitude to you, Beloved Creator and heavenly angels. Thank you, Michael, Raphael, Gabriel, and Uriel! Thank you, Frederique and Pearl! And heartfelt appreciation to Emmet Fox and The Wise Council.

I wish to thank Louise L. Hay for her kindness, wisdom, and love; Reid Tracy, for his warmth, guidance, and support; Jill Kramer, for her incredible intuitive work with words, love, and angels; Christy Salinas, for her artistic and creative talents, as well as her loving nature; Kristina Tracy, for her awesome dedication to spreading the word of God's Love; Margarete Nielsen, for her wonderful and enthusiastic help with my workshops; Barbara Bouse, for her limitless energy and enthusiasm in support of all the Hay House authors and the wonderful Empowering Women conferences; Jeannie Liberati, for her courageous travels inward and outward for tremendously healing purposes; and Ron Tillinghast, for being instrumental in the support of my books and speeches.

I am also grateful to Lisa Kelm, Adrian Eddie Sandoval, Gwen Washington, Drew Bennett, Joe Coburn, Janice Griffin, Polly Tracy, Lynn Collins, Dee Bakker, and everyone else at Hay House.

In addition, I want to thank the seminar coordinators of churches, conferences, and expos that have invited me to speak about communicating with God and the angels. Thank you to Debra Evans, Ken Kaufman, and Gregory Roberts of The Whole Life Expo; Michael Baietti and Mecky Myers of The Health & Life Enrichment Expo; Dr. Carolyn Miller, Dr. Richard Neves, Robert Strouse, Dr. Susan Stevenson, and Dr. Leticia Oliver of the American Institute of Hypnotherapy; Robin Rose and Karen Schieb of The Universal Lightworker's Conference; Shanti Toll and Stella of the Metaphysical Celebration; Ken Harsh of the Universal Light Expo, and many others for giving me the opportunity to commune with the angels of so many people!

A bouquet of gratitude to the editors of metaphysical magazines for their support, love, and light, including David Allikas of *Psychic Advisor;* Donny Walker of *In the Light;* David Young of *The New Times* in Seattle; Gary Beckman and Insiah Vawda Beckman of *The Edge* in Minnesota; Cindy Saul and Gerri Magee of *PhenomeNews* in Michigan; Joe and Shantih Moriarty of *Awakenings* in Laguna Hills, California; Sydney Murray of *Vision* in San Diego; Andrea DeMichalis of *Horizons* in Florida, and the many others who have been instrumental in spreading love and light through the printed word.

PART I

The Healing Messages

❧ Addiction ❧

What is substance, really? Deep in the back of your mind, you remember being in the heart of God. You recall that feeling of total fulfillment, like being in an embryonic sac in your mother's womb. Feeling your wholeness breathing with her breath. That feeling of synchronizing with another is the essence of love that you miss with your heart and your soul.

Substance is a mass of inert energy crystallized into form. In a sense, substance is wooden or lifeless, but in another sense, substance is comprised of remnants of God's love, since the thought-form is but a divine spark of inspiration leading to creation. You who turn to substance to alleviate your loneliness for God are making the choice for a substitute of lesser quality, but nonetheless the same in origin of your original memory of closeness and warmth.

Think of it this way: You are joining with the substance in an internal cuddle with the desire of ending the nightmare of the external movie. You want an internal change that will bring you closer to the heaven you are craving for yourself and your family. Yet, you are choosing an external source to create an internal state. The two can never be reconciled, so you have set yourself up in an impossible situation. You are, in essence, caught in a limbo of eternal frustration because you cannot force the round peg to fit into the square hole, although you try and try again.

Addiction to substance is best burned away in the same eternal flame of desire that originally ignited it. Use the energy of your longing for love to quench your endless cycle of chasing love. Here is how: Ask to build an internal station of

♥ 3

love and light. As you enter your dreams, ask that this flame burn brightly while your subconscious mind takes over for the night. Ask this flame to burn away the dross of your attention; in other words, that which is unneeded in the world.

Your dream time is the best time to ask us to take over, and we will do our best to rearrange your thoughts so that the pyramid of your attention is rebuilt in sequential order. As it is for most of you presently, God is only a small tip of your attention—something you have put as a future priority. We ask and we will help you to rebuild this pyramid so that God comprises the most basic and the biggest rung of your ladder, the basis of your structure and your pyramid. We will help you if you will but make this your intention.

Give us all of your thoughts concerning your addiction. Whether this addiction involves another person or not is of no importance. What we want you to do is give all of your attention to us while we rebuild your thought structure around God and loosen your thoughts around your God-substitute of addiction. We will do this for you if you will let us. But you must hold nothing back, because the entire structure of your thoughts must be rebuilt and reborn in its entirety. If you hold back some thought, say, out of shame, we cannot rebuild the core of your structure.

Give it over entirely to us angels, who even now surround you, and we will construct an empire within you worthy of God and His angels. You will be glad to awaken to dawn with the sunlight bathing your beautiful new structure, built so solidly that there is a glad welcoming of the empty spaces between the pillars. You will no longer desire to fill these empty spaces with substance, because they will instead be filled with light, golden-yellow like the morning sun upon the most promising of days.

❤ ❤ ❤

✄ Anger ✄

When you are hot with lava-red anger within, it would only turn into a smoldering rage were we to tell you to extinguish your true feelings that someone has done you wrong. You feel injured, little one, and who are we to tell you that you are wrong? In truth, you who are a holy child of God are never wrong. However, you may be momentarily mistaken in the perspective you have taken about the truth.

Let us explain: You may have believed that another could take love away from you, or withhold their approval or love of you. This, as you know deep within, is impossible. There is no love to take away from one who shares all holiness with all the world. You are having an argument only within yourself when you feel touched by anger. The lava flows within you over the rocks upon your consciousness, and the hurt and pain seethes with deep sorrow that another could cause you such pain.

"How could they not know how much they are hurting me?" you cry out silently within the chasms of your chest, crying, wanting, desiring for a resolution to your pain. You want the other to know the very depth of your pain. Perhaps you want the other to even feel your pain for but a moment to truly understand the depth of your sorrow.

Yet, again, we emphasize that this battle is with yourself and within your own mind. Do you truly want to live on a battlefield, you holy child of God? Of course you don't, as no angel sent here to earth was ever meant for conflict. You are meant to fly above rage and to see it as if it were a raging river, a flow of constant energy below you, not within you.

You can create a space within you presently where peace can reign. Even if you aren't ready to let go of your rage, you can easily agree to create a pocket of space alongside the anger. See this pocket, like an air pocket under water, dance to its own tune of peace. See it filled with a delightful color like an air bubble swimming in circles in its own playful way. As you delight in this playfulness within you, you may want to visualize yourself swimming inside this bubble in your internal playground.

Feel yourself having fun with the freedom of soaring through your inner space. Take yourself on a wonderful adventure where concerns of safety take a backseat to a sure knowingness that you are eternally safe. Feel how right this freedom seems to you, how natural to be swimming in oceans of safety. When you immerse yourself in this consciousness of freedom, you are also free to choose other thoughts that buoyantly float with play and delight.

Your freedom comes from seeing that you swim through life—not surrounded by sharks—but surrounded by angelfish. You are swimming in circles of like kind, and you are surrounded by others who are exactly as yourself. Have compassion upon those in your circle, knowing that they tread innocently like yourself.

If one or more of those around you occasionally swims in your way, will you forgive them and continue your freedom swim? Or will you become dazed and hypnotized by their seeming lack of order, and allow yourself to become transfixed by the gaze on the past? You want flow and harmony, and this absolutely requires a station of attention on the here and the now.

We are here to help you to bring your dance of life and all your relationships back into divine order and harmony. Look around you with your internal eyes right now, and you will realize that we angels swim with you in perfect harmony like a beautiful school of fish. We are divinely connected by mind thoughts that orchestrate our synchronized movements without effort or concern.

Flow with us ceaselessly, and we will catch your occasional lapses of memory as to your true identity. We will encircle you and guide you in a continuous ballet of glory to God and all mankind.

♥ ♥ ♥

❧ Anxiety ❧

When your mind is focused upon thoughts of the future, it is natural for you to become afraid. You are wanting to peek over the fence of tomorrow, and glimpse into the time just ahead with reassurance that everything will be okay. Let us do this for you, now, oh perfect child of God.

You have no thing about which to worry, and you have our gentle assurance that everything from now until tomorrow is in perfect array. Give us your thoughts about disorder, and we will reorganize them for you until they are captured in a perfect display of faith. You really have no thing to worry about, holy child, as you are master of your day. There is no problem you cannot surmount today or tomorrow, and we are always around you to catch you any time you should fall.

When you were a child and you scraped your knee on a fall on the sidewalk, who do you think it was that pushed your face up toward the sun so that your tears would dry in the kiss of God's love? It was us, dear child, and we shall never leave or forsake you in all your adult lifetime. We can instantly immerse within your thoughts to help you find your way home to heaven.

Should you begin to worry about letting another person down, we ask you to leave those thoughts to us. Could an angel ever let a loved one down? Remember that you are an angel, you holy child of God. You are an angel sent to earth by Him who loves you in His deepest essence. It is impossible that when your thoughts are right and your intentions heart-centered, that you could let a loved one down.

We will support you in all ways, and even when delays are sometimes inevitable and you wonder if God hears your prayers, never fear. We are near. We hold your hand invisibly and guide you to the exact places and people that will cause joy to stir in your heart. Your desire to provide for your family is so sweet and love-based that God hears your prayers no sooner than you have thought of them in your heart.

God, in His own way, weeps for His child's worries. He asks only that you let Him draw nearer and nearer to your heart so that you will recall that you are not alone on this earth. He asks that you allow Him to flow His unearthly love through your heart and bodily vessel, so that you may carry this precious cargo into the marketplace and exchange it for your needs to be met.

The way to heaven is within. You may wonder whether "within" is locked and how you may enter its shelter and safety from the turmoil of life. You need look no farther than your thoughts, my dear. All you need to do to calm the flames of anxiety is to put your intentions upon calmness. Extinguish the belief that anxiety is a sign that you care about a solution. God knows that you care, and He asks that you clear the way for His intervention into your life.

So right now, take three deep breaths and center and clear your mind for us angels to take over. Let us do the driving for a while as you rest your weary mind and body. You work so hard for so long, and you do deserve a rest while we clear your heart of clouds of worry.

If this seems simple—"Just ask"— it is because it *is* that simple! Simplicity is the heart of God, and the answer to your worry. Do not allow your mind to wring itself out of shape by wondering, "What if this happens?" or "What if that happens?" All those "what ifs" are exhausting, and for no good reason!

We, the angels, sing a song of harmony in perfect grace. The reason for the beauty of this song is its simple melody.

Let your mind be in harmony with this melody by concentrating on just one thing: love. Let this be your mantra while you breathe in and out deeply, and feel your mind clear like the sunshine beams away fog.

You are meant to enjoy sunny days free of worry, dear child. Let us wipe away your fears with our gentle hugs. Turn your frets over to us, and we in turn will deliver them to the Creator where you will never see them return to you again. This angelic amnesia is our gift to you, and your freedom from worry is your gift to us.

♥ ♥ ♥

❧ *Arguments* ❧

Are you hurt and exhausted by the heaviness of words heaved back and forth between you and another, dear child? Rest in the corner a moment like a prize fighter, while we mop your brow and fan you with flames of love that leave all anger behind. You are magnificent, dear one, and you are encapsulated beauty in all your days without exception.

Your argument is a duel of battling perceptions, using swords of point-of-view that clash over who is right and who is wrong. You may employ other weapons upon one another, yet like little children fighting with pretend slings and arrows, it is impossible that you could hurt one another, in truth. In fact, the only shadow of a ghost of hurt comes from the moment when you decide to engage in a battle of wits with another. This stems from thoughts of competition in which the "prize" is winning the heralded top of the mound. Yet this prize is, in truth, a prison of loneliness and separation; and the residuals are more hurt and prideful misunderstandings.

Holy child of God, see yourself and the other through eyes of mercy that cry as your egos do battle! See that your loudness of words cannot match the loudness and fury with which your heart cries out for love and assurance. If you can take just one drop of the love we carry to you from God, your heart would be filled to overflowing. You would naturally take this excess of love and have it drip and ooze from your very being so that it touches all that even think of you. Your mere presence in this state of mind next to another person is enough to heal all ill will.

Think about it, dear child: There is another solution, another way to heal this situation that does not require you to inflict additional hurt upon yourself! Isn't this the solution you are even now aching for? God would not leave you without a way to unpaint yourself from the corner in which you now cower in contemplation over what you have done to yourself. You needn't grovel or feel pity for yourself or another, because no child of God is worthy of pity. You merely need to stand up for what is right within you now. By feeling this source of your strength within, you can lead the other person with whom you argued, home. Allow the fleeting memories of your clashing egos to be mere echoes from the battlefield that glint faintly among the merriment of recapturing your youthful knowingness of your true God nature.

There is nothing in truth about which argument can penetrate. The truth is the truth whether anyone dawns upon it or not. You and your friend can argue from now until eternity, but you won't enjoy the truth until you put down your battle instruments and notice your beautiful surroundings. All it takes is for one of you to point to the sunset and say how splendid it is, or to speak of the beautiful mist of the fog or rain dew, and your joint perceptions will be united in agreement.

Think not that you have to lose yourself to win the battle, dear one. You have both already won because, in truth, you never had a way to lose what is rightfully yours. Rejoice in your birthright as a holy child of God, and laugh merrily with all who come your way as you create a delightful place for love and truth to reign freely without restriction of time or place.

♥ ♥ ♥

❧ *Betrayal* ❧

What is at the heart of betrayal, dear one? A feeling of being compromised or unloved? Truly, the person who hurts you is betraying him- or herself alone. This person unwittingly cast a pebble into a pool with ripples that stung you with deep pain instead of a clear reflection of love. Will you now betray yourself further by leaving your true self behind in consciousness? Your focus upon hurt will only serve to further hurt you, precious one. You can do more harm to yourself than any other person by your continually focusing upon this hurt.

Leave the hurt behind, dear child! Do not betray yourself further by walking upon this path of painful contemplation. You do no one justice by holding the hurtful situation in the palm of your hands. And yet you need to heal. So cleansing yourself of hurt will both free your consciousness and rid you of the deep and stinging wound of having a dear one disappoint you.

See now we angels circling around your middle, and notice we are getting closer and gaining in numbers. Our wings are outstretched like one giant circle of a tray around you, and we ask you to place your hands face down upon this tray of wings. Let us warm you from the palms upward with our love. Feel us gliding your energy imbalances to a place of peace and safety with our continuous motion.

You may send your anger at the betrayal from your mind, heart, and gut all the way through your fingers and send it to us. Give us all of your tender and sweet emotions: the love that you feel was taken from you by your friend's betrayal. The feeling of foolishness because you feel you could have known better than to trust this person's sincerity. The feeling that you wasted your time once again on a nowhere relationship. We know just how you feel, dear one.

Yet though we share your hurts and shoulder your burdens, we never lose sight of the fact that in truth, there is no betrayal or hurt. The true heart connection between you and the other person has registered in eternity all the moments of love that it added to the universe. That love, sweet one, can never be undone and never needs to be regretted.

You have done nothing wrong, and you are God's precious child of budding love. Though each of you on earth occasionally stumbles like a toddler taking the first few steps, God and we angels know that your smooth strides are inevitable. You needn't scold yourself or another person for the trips and falls that occasionally occur, even when they seem to be deliberate on another's part.

The consciousness that would cause another to betray you is the same clumsiness that makes babies and little children fall. The inner truth of that person, just as with you, is that the full grasp of love will never lead to competition, manipulation, or betrayal. We ask that you be patient with yourself and others as you all blossom into full emotional maturity.

Be willing to forgive and overlook, dear one, even as you follow your inner guidance that tells you when to keep away from another being on earth. You are put here for a reason, oh holy child of God, and you needn't worry that you must sacrifice your happiness to be in a relationship.

As you heal through forgiveness and clearing releasements, you naturally attract those beings into your life who honor you to the same degree you honor yourself. The rest is natural, dear one, and your path to growth—though laden with trips and stumbles—is a joyous occasion for us to watch. We love you so, and ask that you never forget your true home in heaven in God's heart with us always.

♥ ♥ ♥

❧ *Blame* ❧

Who is there to blame but yourself in this world, and yet ultimately that is not the truth either. A stumbling block of new ones to the path is to place all the blame of the world upon their own shoulders. This is a misunderstanding of the universal law of love. Yes, the cause of all the world is in your mind. However, the solution lies not in self-blame.

Come with us on a journey, dear one, and see yourself from our point of view. Cleanse your negative self-view and know that you are God in disguise as a human. We see you as trying so hard to give, and feeling blocked at every turn. It is as if you are pressing against glass walls that are unyielding, and even now you try so hard to understand our words that you may get a glimpse of heaven even clearer in your heart.

We ask you to stop pressing against the glass wall surrounding you for the moment, and listen with your heart to our words as we speak to you just now. Hear the gentle contemplation and rustling of the wind in your gentle mind and heart. See how holy precious you are as one who only wants what is borne of love. You desire peace, happiness, and a place of rest and safety for your family. You want love and care, and you want to have something to share. These desires are as pure and sweet as a baby lamb, dear one. And if you occasionally twist these desires into ugly contortions of themselves, what is there to care about?

In the ultimate sense, all the pain of leaving your truth for a moment always leads you back to God's care. You see: Everything you do is always from love, for love, and to love. So laugh at the many ways you seek what you already have, and you see how we angels are sometimes amused by your antics. We do wholly care about your trials and triumphs, and we are always with you in all ways.

Still, we ask you to stand back and see our perspective. From the long view, we think you'll agree that there is no thing that you can blame, because there is no thing that can go wrong.

❤ ❤ ❤

❧ *Boredom* ❧

The word *bore* we find interesting in your vocabulary. It means to drill a hole into a thing, does it not? And do you not agree that boredom is akin to feeling emptiness, as if a hole has been bored into you?

The healing comes, then, from asking the emptiness within you this question: "What are you here to teach me?" Remember that emptiness is always filled as soon as the intention becomes clear to fill it. Your choice, then, is the only matter about which to rest your mind. What will you fill it with? Certainly not more of the same that has already led you to boredom.

Invite us in to fill and heal you! Did you know that angels can fly anywhere, including inside bodies and the essence of your souls? We enter where we are invited, so your time will be well spent in gentle contemplation of how to fill yourself up with loving nourishment. Too many beings sit and stew and blame the outside world for their tender feelings. This experience has taught them the futility of outer blame, yet they continue to practice this set of behaviors because they know nothing different.

We are here to tell you, dear, sweet one, that there is a different way to look at boredom. As we have said, your emptiness is filled the moment you *decide* to fill it. We ask you to choose carefully with what you will fill up your emptiness. Your choice comes to you the moment you decide it, because that's how powerful you are.

If you contemplate sorrow, then you have chosen to fill yourself with grief. From our perspective, grief looks like green, stringy vines hanging inside of people's chest cavities like a damp and dreary forest. You probably wouldn't choose it so readily were you to see its sallow colors. These vines make your inner road blocked and difficult, and we know that makes you weary to press on against yourself.

Boredom is simply a messenger brought down to your awareness by your higher self. It is a gift, dear one, and the moment you choose to look at it that way you will laugh in the gentle presence of the place within you where all decisions are made. Look at boredom as you would look upon a roadblock that triggered you to detour to another avenue. You know that where you are bored, something is wrong! And ignoring problems is one way to feel mired in boredom.

You are truly innocent and so much entitled to your feelings, sweet and holy child. Your feelings of boredom lead you gently, if you will let them, to a place where you are wanted and where you want to be. Tug not at boredom, but let it tug at you and you will soon make fast friends with this gentle place within you now.

❤ ❤ ❤

❧ *Breakups* ❧

Occasionally a partnership rips apart at the seam, and this results in two partners floating away from one another while each silently wonders if the breakup was the right thing to do. These *regrets*, more than anything from our vantage point, are what cause the heart to bleed and bear pain. If you make the decision to separate, we ask that you be clear about your reasons and that you surrender the decision then to God. Upon surrender, it is vital that you no longer contemplate or relive the moment of separation, for to do so is to inflict needless pain upon a holy child of God (yourself, the other person, and any of your friends and family who are affected).

Healing from a breakup needn't be painful, though we often see humans experience pain because this is what they expect. Yes, the end of a relationship is a sort of death. And death is always accompanied by grieving. Still, grieving does not have to entail the sort of heavyhearted moaning one always sees in old black-and-white movies. It can be a great time for making resolutions about yourself.

Great changes come out of great sorrow. May we then suggest that you take this opportunity of a breakup—whether one is contemplated, inevitable, or just occurred—and use this vital energy to make a journal entry related to your life? Just write whatever comes to mind that lets you know how far you have traveled, mostly due to this most recent relationship. You will see the value of this partnership, whether it continues or not.

Do you see what a gift you have brought to yourself just now by focusing upon your presents in the presence? There is always another way to see any situation, and we ask that you put all your efforts into kindling good.

❤ ❤ ❤

❧ *Burdens* ❧

Yes, we know you have many heavy burdens upon your shoulders. Would you believe us if we told you that your even heavier burdens are the ones you pull behind you like a mule dragging a plow through thick soil? It is true! Your past, and wreckage from the past that you insist on dragging into the present, are truly your most oppressive sources of resistance to the easy flow of life's gentle grace.

Surrender your burdens, you heavenly angel upon earth! You are much too young to shoulder such a tiresome burden any longer. It robs you of the glory of life, and fatigues you to the point where you do not feel well. Don't think a second longer about your past in any manner such as the person who contemplates which items out of his closet he shall donate to a worthy cause. Donate it all! You don't need a bit of the past, and as long as you believe that you do, your collection of wearisome thoughts will ceaselessly tire you in the present.

When birds fly to a new locale, they don't spend their time wrestling about the trees and countryside they just left. To do so would interfere with their here-and-now process of being fed and sheltered. It is no different for you, dear one. You are being gently guided to allow us to disrobe you of the heavy garments you need no longer carry.

Simply say to the light around you this declaration of your truth and freedom: "I shall no longer carry my past, for it is a burden, and I choose now to lighten my load. I give this past entirely to you, God, and I let go of all impressions of myself borne out of past experiences, now. Today is the day when I release myself and shed away all unneeded skins from days afar. I am free, wholly free, and I needn't worry a bit about this process, for You are here with me."

Your breath can blow away a thousand years of pressure in just one single instant of fully committed release. Push the past out of your body and conscious awareness through your lungs. Breathe, breathe. Blow, blow. Press it out with your single-minded decision to be free. You are your own jail-keeper, sweet angel, and we flutter about you even now in support of your new lightness.

You are becoming one with us in consciousness, and we applaud you for resisting all temptations to return to a burdensome mind-set. Remember that we are here with you in all ways, and we honor your commitment to freedom. We won't interfere, we promise, unless you ask us for help in some way. We only ask that you not wait a moment longer than you need to before calling our name with a single thought or word of, "Angels!" We see you extending yourself far too long before you ask for help, and we stand beside you praying that you will collapse your efforts to withstand so much pressure on your own.

You will soon see that there is no room for burdens in heaven, and the heaven you seek is right here on earth. Share the load with us, dear one, and you will easily be lifted of a weight you may not even know you carry. We ask you to lighten your life on behalf of all the other earthly angels who need you.

❤ ❤ ❤

❧ *Burnout* ❧

What could be scarier than to not like your job and not see any way out of this mental trap? So many of you find yourselves in this position that we are creating an entire chapter on this topic. From where we are, we see burnout as a cry for help and attention from your emotional body. Just as your physical body tells you something is wrong when it cries out in pain, so too does your emotional body give you clear signals.

Now what do you suppose your emotional body is trying to tell you with this feeling you call "burnout"? Of course, you know that it means some changes are necessary in your work life. Did you know that you can make these changes and still be 100 percent safe? It is true! You needn't hesitate in listening to your emotional body because you believe your situation is futile. We are here to guard you in all ways, including the transition of making your career match your expectations of yourself.

Let's put it this way: When you suffer in silence about your job, you are blocking the flow of light into the world. You are meant to be a great healer in whatever capacity your career takes you. When you seek to stifle your emotional body's cries, it feels rejected like a little child, abandoned and unloved. So you can see why it throws a fit and finally gives up. This giving-up is the dead feeling accompanying burnout, and it is tragic indeed.

It is also useless to try and fight it. Your dead-horse emotional body has gone to sleep like a numb arm that you slept upon too long. You can only revive this part of yourself by rolling over to the other side and rubbing your arm. Your emotional body comes back to life when you stop sitting on top of it, when you roll over and give it some attention.

We'd like you to spend some time alone in gentle contemplation with yourself, dear one. We'd like you to have a notebook ready because the ideas will flow, and we want you to capture them on paper. We are here to support you, and one way we want to reassure you is that everything will get better. *When?* you ask. As soon as you want it to, we answer. Will you—that is, the little you that walks around all day—stand aside and allow your inner self some air time? Is this not fair from the being whom you expect to pleasure you, and whom you pummel the moment this being becomes depressed?

Yes, it is fair to allow your emotional body to vent some of its trapped energies. You needn't decide that you will follow this being's guidance just yet, so please don't think we are asking for your full commitment in shifting your life to suit your emotional body. You are better off simply making an appointment to hear out your inner self, who has much to tell you.

Together, the two of you can work out a compromise agreement so that both of your needs can be met. Usually, this means that you will ask for a slow and safe change of events, and your emotional body will be relieved to be heard, and that change is coming. The two of you are friends, dear one, and you needn't part as enemies through burnout.

❤ ❤ ❤

❧ *Career* ❧

We think the word *inspiration* is integral here, because you can get inspired about what kind of career will bring you joy. We say "joy," because that's what a career is all about. You are a drop of sunshine sent here to kiss the earth's morning dew. Imagine the joy the sunshine receives as it radiates outward in extension of God's eternal glow. Now you will see why we mention joy so early in this discussion of career.

So many of you have decided that you are up against a wall with your career and that you are "held up" by outside forces that govern your choices. Dear children, nothing could be further from the truth! We wish you could see yourselves from our perspective, where we watch dear children giving up their perfect freedom. It is tragic indeed to see so many of you trapped in jobs that suffocate your very essence of joy.

You don't have to stay where you are unwanted, dear ones. Release yourself in mind first from a job that cannot hold you, and see your body soon be released in turn. Hold this in your hearts, especially as you go to bed each night: "I have nothing to fear. I make the choice to hold my joy in mind as I think of my career." Do just this and you will feel a jump and shift in your consciousness, dear ones.

Your readiness to seek the career of your choice is the next thing we will address. Many of you dream of the day in the *future* when you will be made ready and prepared for your consciously chosen career. In our opinion, this is a mistake in consciousness. We ask you to stay grounded in the day that you are in now as you think of the career. In this way, you bring your dawn to you now, instead of the next day.

Do you know what we ask? We are saying to stay in the moment with your wishes, and as you contemplate your next movement, say to yourself that it is at *this* moment when change occurs. Not next, not never. But now. Congratulate yourself for staying on top of this truth, because it is very difficult for mortals to see. But we ask you to learn this for yourself and then teach it to others, because we must pass this one along.

So many are seeing their jobs through the sight of a child who says, "When I grow up, I'll be this or that." This means of consciousness never leaves most adults who continue, well into their older ages, to see careers from this future orientation.

Today is the day, and now is the time! There has never been a better day for you to be grounded in thoughts of your right career. And what is this career? Well, we have left this important part for now, because it is at this moment after making the conscious decision of now, that we get to this next part of how.

Of course you know, or try to know, that your career is the essence of your giving being. As you extend outward like the sun's radiation energy, you are giving of yourself outward. You are actually growing in size and radiation as you give of yourself. And you receive, too, in the blink of the eye of the pulsating giving and receiving rays of the sun. See this in your mind's eye, and you will get a glimmer of what a career is all about.

A sun cannot pretend to be a moon or vice versa. Know what are you essentially, and you will know what you automatically send and receive. You must radiate your natural qualities, and many of you are not aware of these beauties within you because you have not yet taken time to *list them.*

We urge you to do so, and as you list these qualities, feel them spreading outward from within you.

This is your career, to shine outward always in ever-creative ways. Your artistic abilities are shining even now as you think about this. Imagine what you can do once you contemplate them even further. You have the essential ingredients to paint a magnificent picture around you, in whatever fashion suits you. We support you in all ways that it takes for you to be in your natural self, extending and pulsating outward beautifully, like the ray of the sun whom you are.

You are your greatest asset, and you seek to "employ" or use yourself to the highest degree possible. That is admirable, dear one, and we seek to assist you in this endeavor. Rather than call you by name in assembling your employment, we shepherd you in ways that will tend the larger flock. We gather 'round you in our midst and give you our blessings, which are our greatest means of elevating you and your surroundings to the highest ideals.

You see, it is not on the material plane where we are most effective. Yet, our effect affects the material plane very profoundly through your shifting of awareness upon your heavenly duties. In every interaction with another, call upon your heart to teach him about the LOVE that is within him. For that is your job, dear child. Help one another to get past the crying out of His holy name, and get onto the realization that His love resides within us all.

The tenderness of the mercy that you show to a brother will shower you with a resonance that is impenetrable by any darkness. For no darkness can reside within the joy once its light is awakened. Your beam radiating strongly from your heart into his, is enough to alert your brother to his sleeping holiness. Use not words, but a smile. Seek not action, but a thought instead. Capture your attention upon the light within us all, and see its magnificence grow within your holy sight. For you are the light upon the hill that shines to all brothers who would seek for this sustenance.

Do you then see that the form of employment is secondary to this outward reaching? Now in this minute are you able to heal a brother of anything that may frighten him! You are wholly capable of erasing all bad feelings that capture the hearts of another. *Use* your power, dear one! And use it well!

Be not afraid to swell in love for one another. Your magnificence is greatest as you open wide your heart and encircle each being with loving eyes, just as we angels who look upon each of you and see but glory in who you are. For our jobs and your job are one in the light and the greatness that is God before and within us. The mighty mountain you seek to climb is beneath your feet this very moment, dearest being. And as you stand trembling with the energy of determination, lose not sight that this is the moment that is pinnacle above all the others. There is no more precious moment in which to embrace a brother than now.

♥ ♥ ♥

❧ *Changes* ❧

When the autumn leaves fall, do you cry at the change in the season? Perhaps, just a little. Too soon the earth seems to change before you are ready, and the seasons shift without asking anyone's permission!

Do you feel the earth shaking below your feet as though your life was trembling with rippling fear? Do you feel shaken by confusion over which direction to take? Changes are coming into your life and you feel out of control over containing them. You also feel undecided about which route and avenues to take for your desired outcome. Worry not, dear soul. You have come to the right source for which to unburden yourself.

You see these changes as giving pause and interrupting your flow of events. We see the changes as the flow of energy beneath your feet as you are propelled into motion. The flowing river changes endlessly as it carries a boat upon its back. The changing motion of your life is doing much the same, sweet one, as it carries you safely and swiftly across some spots of life you wouldn't have liked to tarry upon. For you see, beneath the raging river are craggy rocks that—were you to stop and ponder your options awhile—you may have become snagged upon.

So give thanks for the swiftness with which your life now changes directions, and for heaven's sake, don't impede its flow. For you never know which moments you hesitate or resist may land you upon some rock below the surface.

Caution is given you from within when you need it, and you can readily trust this riverboat guide on your safe passage to the far banks in unknown places. Remember that your guide has been on this river in many lives and in many times. Although it seems unfamiliar and uncharted to you, your guide is quite comfortable and at home. Perhaps it's time for you to hole up in your cabin and enjoy the ride.

There is a sweetness within the temporary turmoil as you float down the river, and none so gentle as the rocking of the sweet earth mother's song as she cradles you within her ever-steady motion. Your rhythms of life are now unconstricting and are becoming more natural. Do not be alarmed at the changes going on within you and in your life. Every moment of the ride, you are in full capacity to shift your weight a bit to the side, and so steer the course ever so slightly.

So you see that you *do* have control, through your thought and intention. The control comes from gentle decisions, dear one. Just as a child caught in a riptide becomes endangered if she panics and fights against the water's pull, you also find your safety and power from relaxing and knowing that you have all the options you want within your mind. Use that power with grace, little one.

Remember Who your creator is, and how He thrusts onto you an equal measure of creative power. You have no need to fear your own power, for it is eternally part of you. What we are saying is that resisting changes is a power-less way to control your life. But making a firm decision is a power-full way that never fails. Use your power with grace! We urge you to be in charge of your faculties, as you co-create with heaven. You are in charge. Yes, you truly are.

The decision is yours, and so our question to you is this: "What do you want?" Perhaps you are unhappy with the changes occurring around and within you because they represent that which you do not wish to see within yourself. Is your inner you spilling out and pouring into your outside world? Instead of crying at this occurrence, you can use this as your chance to mop it up inside and outside. In that respect, the change is always good news. Change is always for the better. You needn't resist; you only need change your mind, and you will capture your life flow like a tamed river.

❤ ❤ ❤

❧ Child Abuse ❧

We have seen many of our little ones getting hurt in many ways, and we would like this to stop. Our heart energy soothes the little ones who needlessly suffer at the hands of fearful adults. Yet we know our sympathy will only add to the rage, and so we offer you another solution.

Did you know that if you stop and pray once an hour, "A solution will be done," that you pause the time in which the darkness pretends to be the light? You pierce the veil of darkness and reveal its truth to light so that it pales into a faded background where sweet tones of music shine forth in gladness, with all hands clasped in one circle of friendship.

Do not delay this undertaking, for we support you from the heavens to watch over and guide your prayers for the children. Even still, a mere handshake from heaven is not enough to unearth the very being behind this cruelty to our children. We need testaments from ones who, like you, care so deeply for the children that their hearts are frozen with indecision about, "Whom shall we help?" and "What shall I do?"

Move forward with grace and unity away from this indecision that paralyzes your actions from stemming forth from the love that is inside you. We are calling you to action, not from an angry heart, but from a heart so filled with love that it melts the darkness within those who would hurt the children.

Do you know what we say, dear one? We are calling you to our hearts so that we may gather together all souls concerned in one united effort to heal away the cause of this hardship. There is no solution on earth to end the suffering of millions of children, so we ask you to turn away from inspecting the suffering in hopes that this will lead you to its cure. It only brings more suffering when you study it, precious children of our Holy Creator!

Do not seek to cure ills with your close inspections. Turn inward instead to One Who knows all answers. He calls you to gather at His side and turn all ills and cares over to His loving grace. As He ferrets out decisions and calls you to grace your abilities with action, you needn't hesitate in inaction as you wonder if His call was mistaken. God makes no mistakes, and He knows fully of what you are capable at this moment!

Be in gladness as the Creator incorporates your loving being into His mighty plan to end all suffering upon the earth. He is magnificent, and you are His greatest miracle. You mustn't prolong the sadness an instant longer by investigating whether the call to greatness within you is or is not the genuine article. Trust that it is, and you will feel enveloped in the mighty love that enfolds you even now.

You uncover your greatness, which is the cause of healing all humanly mistakes, as you uncloak your eyes from the blindness that hides you from the awareness of His love. Make no further mistakes with these precious children whom He leaves in your care, dear ones. You are called to shepherd them in the way that He points for you.

Ask Him to direct you for the social change that fuels your passion. He is the instrument of healing, and you are His social cause. You are the fuel that gives love to many parents and that heals their hearts from the fear and brings them solace. Heal their fear and guilt, so that they too may drop to their knees in awe of the Magnificent One who greatly loves them. Abandon your judgments with haste so that light may flow through you, and flood all with whom you speak.

You are not to direct this healing flow in any way but the way which nature intends for you. You are simply asked to draw back the curtains that contain and seal the light within you, and become like a clear-paned window that indiscriminately allows the sunlight to radiate through to all who would touch and see it. You are a window to God for all who seek Him, dear one, and your shepherding skills are innately yours. Allow them to shine as you bring others to His light so that they may heal and thus bring forth the love to their children.

All is healed now in this instant that we come before Him. Let us sing in unison, "Hallelujah, Hallelujah, His mighty will is in loving service to all."

♥ ♥ ♥

❧ *Children* ❧

Precious little ones are gifts to you, in strangers, in blood, and in all. We seek to unite you in their laughter, and we urge you who have sought for inner peace to listen for the utterance of a child, which will bring you home to your heavenly ways. You are refreshed in their laughter and gaiety, so you needn't see childlike play as annoyances that interrupt the important duties of the day.

In effect, their laughter is a release from the stringent tightness that threatens to strangle your body and your mind. You become tight during days when you pretend to like that which you actually abhor, and your breathing becomes shallow and uneven. Do not discount what this lack of oxygen does to your cells, precious child! We urge you to relax from tightness and to learn of a child's ways, which will lead you in directions from which your air-force can more steadily flow in relief and harmony.

There are contagions in the world thought that promote disharmony. Children know not of these factors, as their minds are still fresh from the heavenly home. Allow their mind-set to take over your awareness for a little while, and feel the refreshment course through your body as it brings you home. Their natural curiosity may lead you to inspect a caterpillar at close distance. Notice how its fuzzy little feet bounce gaily upon the loam, and the gentle way it cuddles and crawls.

Do not lose this ability to gaze fondly upon nature, precious one. We urge you to heighten your awareness of the natural wonders around you. It is this healing message that children urgently bring you from the Creator. They cast their reminders upon you daily, yet how often do you see them as signals for your annoyance? Do not shirk off children's innocence as worthless, as they are our most helpful teachers upon the earth.

Do you see what we are after here? A complete reversal in the order in which you place upon other persons. There is great value upon the world's order of teachers, which, in fact, is in reverse. There are teachers of many sorts, that is true. But the greatest teachers of them all are fresh from heaven, and they bring with them the triumphant song of grace and wonder. They are awed by simplicity; a value that you can learn to do on your own.

Use the children as your sure witnesses to God's wonder and grace, dear one, and you shan't go wrong as you circle and climb upon paths of greatness in your lifetime on this earth. Their wings may be folded from your sight. But you have our assurance that the little ones are mighty angels sent for your assistance upon your emerging planet. They bring you wondrous gifts, if you will but sit a moment and chat with a child and use your open willingness to see in a new way.

Are you asking us if children should intervene upon the politics and policies you have upon this great earth? Certainly we see room for such an intervention, but with practical considerations melded with their gentle, innocent wisdom. You would do well to consult a child before making a new law, and to ask the child's point of view about items of great importance.

You will hear, in the child's very breath, a gentle love that points to a bountiful profundity of wisdom. Allow the child's sweet power to sweep all dissonance away. Remember that they are fresh from the Creator and have not yet allowed themselves to lose His lessons, as many of you who have been here longer already have.

Replenish yourself from the well of His fountain by the

grace of His heavenly angels whom you call "children" upon this earth. God be with you in all ways, for we place His mighty sword of wisdom into your hearts as you are called upon into action on behalf of all children everywhere. The fight is not within your home, but within your heart. Surrender it to God, and you will find victory everywhere He is. And He is here, even now, dear one. He is in your heart and in your home. Trust in the Love, and you shall not be pulled apart by any faction in any time, precious and holy child of God. You are loved. Remember that always.

♥ ♥ ♥

❧ Communication ❧

As a tool of communication, speech is a poor substitute for the heart and eyes. We are leaning upon many of you to awaken these uncovered tools in glad awareness of all that they offer to you. First, if you awaken your heart energy and uncover this as the tool that it is, you will find yourself connecting much quicker to those around you.

There is an unconscious energy between all people, no matter what brings them together. Perhaps you have been aware of this "shadow conversation" that follows your outward conversation. Listen in on the shadow conversation with your inward ear, and you will hear another side of your relationship with others. The honest truth is spoken here at this level, as one child to another who holds nothing in secret from the other.

This is what you may refer to as "the heart of the matter," because it truly is central to all your dealings with other people. You may, then, want to monitor not only what is received in these silent conversations, but also what it is you put into this flowing bloodstream of invisible energy between you. Watch what thoughts you drop into this bloodstream, as they are rapidly carried to another and received at the level of conscious truth. Your thoughts of daggers or of swords are received as painful tugging at the ears of the other. Your envisionings of love are received as such.

Enter this flow of conversation as it already exists, and eavesdrop upon your silent self speaking to another. You may be amazed at what you hear, but doubt it not, for it will guide you in silent truth to another who is like you. Have compassion upon yourself and another as you hear the cries of the heart that are spoken at this level. The conversation is there, and if you are aware, you will hear it at the level at which it is spoken around you right now.

❤ ❤ ❤

❧ Crime ❧

We wanted to talk to you about crime from the perspective of safety. We know that many in your world want to shield yourselves from crime, and we have some answers. Release your need for safety, and relax. The world is contemplative right now, and we bring you into safety through your receptivity, not your tension.

Passion is the heart of crime; it's a soul stirring with no feeling of escape. This creates a tremendous energy that is visible to all in The Angelic Realm. Believe us that we will warn you if we see a thunderstorm of this magnitude coming your way. Yet, through your tension—though you believe it to be a raincoat against torrential rains of negative activity—it actually makes you drenched with it.

We cannot permeate your shell with our warnings, so do you see that your best defense against criminal activity during these shifting times is to have no defense at all? We know this seems illogical in your world, and it is certainly paradoxical unless you consider the unseen world through our eyes.

The colors of dark criminal activity are so vivid that we act like forest rangers spotting fires in the distance. We see pockets of safety, and we keep you there while the world is madly adjusting to its new spiritual speed and realm. There will be fires burning bright, and as you reawaken your spiritual sight, you will see them along with us.

Do not become casual about crimes, yet do not overadjust your life in preparation for crime, either. For, whatever you expect is bound to happen, and we will always bring you to safety. You do us a great service, therefore, whenever you purge your mind of worries and fears about perceived dangers in store for you. You do not want to draw negative energy to you, so do not cast your line in the water trolling for it. Throw it back, if you've already caught it!

What we mean, dear one, is this: Do not in any way clutch dearly to thoughts about your physical safety. We do look out for you day and night. That is part of our job. Yet, you do yourself much disservice when you clench your jaws and brace for unsafety in the world.

Dear one, please learn that the world but reflects your wishes! Would you wish for danger? No, of course you would not. Then we implore you to rid your mind of thoughts of safety, for you do not know the power of your mind in this regard. You are like little children playing with a powder keg, not knowing the danger you bring yourself every time you contemplate the question, "Am I safe?" For we see black smoke released from your mind when you pose such questions, and this smoke is a signal that draws forth the very thing that you fear.

We do not tell you this to scare you further, dear one. But we realize that you must know how much power your mind has given you to draw anything you contemplate at a moment's notice. For this, you can be grateful, though. God would not give you any gift that you could truly misfire. Though you may, in fact, draw great danger to yourselves with your thoughts, it is merely child's mischief in the whole scheme of things.

For you see, gentle spirit, that you are not in any grave or mortal danger in your truest essence. That part which detaches from the body is the true makeup of who you are, and even now this part of you giggles at the preposterous question of its own safety. There is no danger that can be posed to this gentle giant within each of you.

You are sleeping, resting comfortably within the very shell

of God's heart. And He would see that nothing can harm you, not now, not ever. Rest well, sweet one, as we gently sing you lullabies that free your mind of worries, cares, and all contemplations that are not of heaven or of your true home.

♥ ♥ ♥

❧ *Dating* ❧

When you go out on the town, do you know that you bring one or more of us along? We love to see love, and we will gladly intervene—when asked—to keep the transitional love flowing along smoothly. We realize your dates can be anxious affairs. Rest assured that we are here to help you, not only in The Angelic Realm, but beyond.

We can assist you in getting to the heart of the matter with your date quite quickly, so you will know without doubt whether this is a being you would want to spend time with. Ask us to show you—we'll help to guide the right words out of your mouth so you can adjust your frame of reference with this other person right away.

Your countenance upon a date is an outward focus, and we try to draw you inward instead. Think of a flower. Its petals are its beauty, but the beautiful petals draw from the lifespring deep within the flower's core. Your core upon a date, centered within your own wellspring of healing and eternal energy, is the fragrance that attracts love to you on even your first date. Allow your fragrance to be cast upon the wind around you, mindful only of your inner essence of joy.

What we are saying, dear reader, is to cast away all cares, worries, and concerns that are along this line: "How do I look?" "What shall I say?" and "What will it cost?" Put your cares into your center core where they will dissolve away. Your eternal attractiveness is assured within this central point of your being, dear one.

We ask you to withhold your fears and put your intent inward upon your date. We are not asking you to become reclusive or introverted. Not at all! Your internal frame of reference will bring you sparkling conversation and immense joy with others, be it a date or other social setting. We see those of you enjoying yourselves the most, who are staying centered in this sacred space while in the company of others.

We ask not that you become disinterested in others' welfare, but that you stay centered in your own true space of being where your interest naturally bubbles up in authenticity. What we mean to say is this: Your essence is charming, and you needn't worry that you would lapse into a being that bores or repels others.

The others in your group and on your date are conversing with you on the invisible plane, and they know when you are being truthful or not. The true attractiveness of your honesty is unforgettable, and you needn't trust us on this one. Try it alone, and then ask us to help you, and watch how others react.

With us, your spirit swells attractively, and you bring with you into any conversation a third ingredient that adds a delightful dimension to the room. Others will become vividly attracted to your every word without knowing why. Your ingredient is the invisible essence of spirit, dear one, and you are asked to bring it to every being with whom you interact.

Your gift of swollen spirit is an unmistakable one, that awakens others to their long-forgotten hunger to reconnect with who they are. You are a catalyst for change, dear one, whether you are on a date, at a grocery store or bank, or standing in a long line. Use your time wisely for the sake of spirit, and all your relationships will turn out healed. Remember, you are not alone.

Granted, we may come along with you on your date, but you can also block us out at any time you choose. We are mute when anger is in the air, for instance. We are made invisible whenever frustration hits the air. So you choose and you are in control. You tell us where we can help you along, and we gladly do this in exchange for seeing your happiness, dear child. We are meant to help you along on this earth, and when coupling occurs on a date setting, we sing in the heavens with music and laughter. We want to help!

♥ ♥ ♥

⚘ Death ⚘

Departing from this earthplane is one of life's early lessons. You do it so often that one would think you would be adjusted to it by now. Apparently you forget some of your earlier lessons so that you may encounter some later ones. This is fine, because this is God's law. Some of you remember leaving the earth plane in earlier years, and this leaves room for some of the rest of you to catch up on all the news about what is after this life.

One thing is sure: You will not be needing this body in the afterplane. We help you to adjust to a new, ready-made body that fits your skin better than any earthplane body! We inject humor to help you see this transition called "death" in a new light. You needn't fear this change, dear one. It is coming. That is inevitable. And we can help you prepare for this transition in such a way that your earthplane life is not interfered with.

We see people who are here on earth contemplating the afterlife. We wish them well, and we see them as seekers of the truth and light. But we caution them to return to an earlier, innocent, and childlike focus of the earthplane.

Do not be so concerned about, "What is after this life?" We will tell you all that you need to know, but not so much that your time left here on earth is ruined. If we were to tell a starving man about all the delicious delicacies awaiting him someday when he gets to a restaurant, that would be cruel. The rest of his days when he is not in the restaurant would be ruined in anticipation of what is next.

We ask that you do much the same and focus on what is here for you now. There is so much to gather and share here on the earthplane, dear children! Do not let the surprise of what is in store for you be anything but a glimpse of your focus. Do not be overrun with thoughts of heaven, for you do have access to it while you are here on the earth. Life will take care of itself, if you will let it.

Things will not be that much better for you in the afterlife plane if you waste your life thinking about your future in heaven. Of that you can be sure. Just think of the joy you will feel in reviewing your solid gold life spent in service to your siblings here on earth. Then compare that to a life spent in future contemplation and without dutiful action.

There is joy in giving, dear one! Do not believe us, but simply try it for yourself and see. This is the essence, the bloodstream of life. The desire to serve comes masked in many ways, and one of them is the obsession with death and heaven. You think you become an angel when you get here, but the truth is that you are right now called to perform heavenly acts while among those upon the earth. You can do it. You can give so much, even when you believe you have so little to give.

Dear one, how can we convince you of the rightness of God's plan? You needn't take our word for it, but we do need to push you just a little to tip you in the right direction. Give service in whatever way feels comfortable to you, and you will fear death just a little bit less. Then give each day, and watch all cares about death dissolve and then vanish.

❤ ❤ ❤

❧ *Depression* ❧

We are nearby when you are downtrodden. We glimpse your sadness, not to understand it, but to revel in your glowing, which does seem to burn brighter once you turn your yearnings for love inward. You turn inward upon yourself in sadness and end up in revelation, from which gladness is born.

Your wiseness in using this energy to feed upon yourself is engendered with sweetness. For, at times in which you turn inward to lick your wounds, we gently cradle your soul in our wings and hold you even when you will not feel our presence encircling you. You shut us out, yet there is a knowingness that your call to us for help has been met.

And though you long to review the stinging of salt within your wounds, we give you flowers of gladness that pull you out of your sorrow and into your heaven within. So when your emotions seesaw, know that this is your glory being revealed amidst the clouds you feel are within you. You, at times, long for the clouds to cover you in sadness so that you may spend moments cloaked away from darkness. You use your sadness as a means of escaping from the world you choose to see as cruel and demanding.

We applaud your grace in turning inward, sweet child of heaven. Yet, turn inward whenever it beckons to you! There is no better moment than now for you to return to your refreshing pause that is but a moment away. Whether in sadness or in brightness, refresh yourself often as you drink from your inner well.

Your time is of your own making, and we nurture you gladly from whatever standpoint you take. We give you this push, though: That sadness is just as easy to choose as is the shining light. We don't discount your sorrows. We merely seek for you a way of joy, as your shining beacon beckons others to come hurriedly out of the storm into their own inner sanctums of shelter.

Use your beacon to shine warmth onto other lives, and feel your own coldness melt briskly away. You are a haven from the storm for others, and your greatest moments of glory are used as a lighthouse for smiling souls. Your name is written upon heaven as a shining example of those who have similar sorrows. Use the momentum of the storm to gain strength. Feel the pulsing storm push you further in your life, giving you courage and expansion.

Your respite of depression is used wisely indeed, when it leaves you feeling resolved to be your own captor no longer. We see you breaking free from the encircling of darkness and leaving the prison walls so gladly behind. The applause of the thunderstorms cannot scare you when you put it into this context.

Your breath is the life force that propels you to find a gentler breeze. Your surroundings are but mirrors of your choices, dear one, and your gentler days are coming to you even still. There is no way for us to settle into your patterns if you would hold us at bay. Use our flutters to open the wings of your heart, and feel the light come flooding in, although you may fear more pain of darkness.

Your choice is the essence of the direction in which your life is leading you. Think not that victimhood is upon you, for you have been the captor of your own very soul, and you are the releaser that frees every being with whom you come in contact. Choose freedom, then, for everyone, and you choose freedom for yourself.

And on this bright day, your glory can be seen for miles

away. For you are a shining example, and let others see this blaze of freedom upon you. You are the freedom that others now seek! Set no weights upon yourself, in thought that such weight would earn you glory. They but delay you, so do no more self-penance.

The blues that you call depression are but an inverted way of looking at the world. The honor that you seek is upon you now, and you needn't push or force it. Yet, seek glory not for yourself, but in all things seek glory only for God, and you shall see your name scripted across the heaven in His name forever.

Seek honor not, then, in depression—which means a burrow in the ground. Stand upon the mountain of discovery and give credence to His name that is within you. Let no man see you stand upon anything but this hallowed ground, and give rise to honor by leading men with your beacon. In this, there is no capture.

♥ ♥ ♥

❧ *Desire* ❧

"I shan't want for anything" is the solemn vow that you took upon your plunge into the human castings. Yet, the earth-shattering realization upon your awakening in the human flesh shook you to your very soul with revelations that you were responsible for self-feeding. This took you back, to a time long ago, when your very being recalled moments of despair. You wrapped this past time and brought it forward into present memory and laid the time recalls one across the other.

The past is splattering the present with desires for pleasures of the earthly flesh. Dear one, do not think we seek to cast shadows upon your earthly garden. Yet, the time has come when we ask you to rethink your desires in the light of what you *truly* want while you are upon the earth. We implore you to reconsider some of your assumptions about what it is you need. Do you truly believe the child of God could amass a wealth of fortune to take home to the Father as a child seeking a parent's approval?

What is it that you truly want, dearest one? Think long and hard upon this question, and you will turn inward and soon find the wealth that is within you. For you *are* a fortune of treasure, a glittering treasure chest that can multiply as many times as you feel able. Use your good fortune for the help of multitudes who will find you the instant you make this decision within yourself: "I am ready to supply the earth's needs with my riches. I seize upon my wealth within and give freely as I am replenished."

Dear heavenly child upon the earth, the joy that awaits this decision is immeasurable compared to any earthly desires.

Give freely of your treasure within, and delight in the play that now comes your way! See the eyes cast heavenward as you laugh and smile with others who seek you out. Fear not that you shall exhaust your supply, for our Heavenly Creator gives as freely as you do of His own treasurehouse of good.

You are the wealth that the world seeks even now, and as you open your vaults to the others, you suddenly see your own worth. Your instrument of peace multiplies as you share it, and your storehouse overflows with ripe fruit for all who would seek its solace. Hold back from no one, but give freely of the love that is yours to share. Flow the light freely from within and without, as it passes through your life in steady stream.

We bid you to share in this secret: that there is but one desire that you possess, and this desire has already been met. Seek this greatest of treasures in its glorious surroundings, and you will find yourself even as you do. For you are the heavenly riches that God has promised to us all, and as you let us give to you, we seek no greater riches than what He has in store. For heaven is here, and we pass among you its seedlings of joy. Revel in its majesty, dear one, and drink upon its joy.

Live in gladness that this is so, and you will feel the stamp of quenched desires upon your brow. And in this simple quenching, you find that which all of your siblings know: that you and we are one upon His heart. One glorious child of God glittering in millions of shining reflections like the facets of one jewel casting light in multiple directions from one Source. This jewel that is you!

❤ ❤ ❤

❧ *Direction* ❧

Do you feel lost at times, sweet child? You do at times struggle to find your way, yet we stand ready to beckon you home at any time you would call for our directions. Your guidance, which places one foot surely before the other, will serve you all of your days. There is no time when your guidance is lost, yet there are times when you shield yourself from knowing its course.

You doubt and switch between the steady gate of God's direction and the circling of backtracking upon yourself. As you think you are moving forward, you become disheartened upon seeing a sign of a familiar trail that signals that you have doubled back and lost your way. This is the time to sit down and not fight against yourself, for those who struggle against being lost get farther away from the trail. But the being who sits, breathes, and gazes awhile soon finds recomposure. And this resolves the dilemma of being far from the trail, in time for the sunset to lead him home.

There is no time when you are lost, dear one, though signs can seem to point in different directions and confuse you further still. You shift in consciousness from one level to the next, and you worry at the awareness of this loss in focus. Do no further harm to yourself, dear one, by contemplating your "lostness" at the edge of the forest. For we will lead you back in perfect time.

There are others among you lost upon the trail, and at times you lead one another in circles going nowhere. As you cast about in sorrow, contemplating where you are going, do you ever surmise an inner voice that would lead you home? We teach you of this ready compass and offer you a chance to check its gauge. For when you let it lead you out of darkness, you trust its readiness to guide you surefootedly in troubled times. The compass is in perfect order at all times, dear one! Use it often, and it will guide you always, sure and sure.

Perhaps you do not take the time to check it frequently, and only use it when you are far away off the trail. This is also wise, as it proves to you its reliability. We are urging you to use it frequently, for in it is your Creator's wisdom, which He has packed as gear for you.

Some of you who wonder about this gauge and wish to discover its many uses, please hear this: We will gladly teach you of its presence, if you will ask us. Sit quietly in contemplation, and imagine us coming near you. As we enter into your heart with a language of feelings, use your inner ear to decipher the message that answers your questions with knowingness.

You will know we are near by our presence, which sends signals to your mind. These signals you can choose to disregard as imagination. Yet, we will draw nearer to anyone who calls us, and our warmth, we believe, is unmistakable for another presence. Ask us to show you this compass that we call "home," and we will gladly teach you its operation. For it is our honor to share in the gladness that comes from fully being a witness to the love that is within us all.

♥ ♥ ♥

❦ *Disappointment* ❦

Does it sometimes seem hard to honor yourself when others guard their hearts in ways that disappoint you? Believe us that we do understand your sorrow with human behavior, as we have seen choices that we would not have made for you if we were asked. Yet, we still see the glowing goodness within each of you.

We know how close you all are to making the greatest of discoveries about yourselves! We cheer you on in times of sorrow, even when the end seems a very long time off. You are closer than you know to a time of monumental discovery, dear one, and we ask you to cling to hope along with us. For that faith will take you farther than any one human could ask you to go.

But it doesn't seem simple, does it? Perhaps you achieved a level that you hoped would reward you, yet the offering did not come. You feel downtrodden as if others had walked across your very back, ignoring the pain that is beneath their feet. You may feel useless and unworthy of the honor that we tell you is due you. Yet, there is a simple truth that is healing in this concern.

There is a risk in telling you this, yet we believe it is in your best interest to hear this: There is nothing coming to you tomorrow that you do not already have in your hearts today. So that when you seek for your goodness in tomorrow's agenda, you are always disappointed. Because the flowing that you seek is already here, in completion, darling one!

Think not that tomorrow can add to your completeness, for that would be an impossible feat. There is nothing to add to one who knows no need, such as yourself. What could be added to you tomorrow that you do not already have?

Perhaps you think you need something that is not presently within you. We ask you: What could this be? What seeming item did God not give to you, or could He not bestow upon you in this moment in which you reside now? Think not that another needs to add a thing unto you, or enrich you with an encircling that you lack in the present. For you have already earned your creation, and your Creator has promised you all the rest.

For some, there is a thought of past times that cause them to stir in guilt and unworthiness. Yet, even these beliefs are not enough to hold off God's riches! For no mortal on earth could cease the Heavenly Creator's riches from coming in steady streams for now and forever more. So we ask you to delight and dance upon these blessings that are with you as we speak. Your joy sends light-filled messages to the One who is in heaven with you. And your joy is His.

Yes, it is safe to let go of your prescriptions of what you think is due to you. These appointments that you make as scripts in context for others always lead to dis-appointments. For God casts others to you as surely as He casts you to others. Allow the others their breathing space to be as they will be, and nothing can disappointment you of their making. And as your needs are ready-met, so are others spilling over with the treasures of heaven that they can also offer you. So do you see your sharing, which is within you all!

♥ ♥ ♥

❧ *Dreams* ❧

Y ou speak of the term *sweet dreams* as if to differentiate
them from the rest. The garden of your thoughts grows
wildly at times, and its nature can seem to bloom perennials
that capture your full attention. What is this period of time
you call "dreams," but an opportunity to flourish in the wild
expanses of your inner atrium? Your mind, which seems darkened in the light but harbors a perfect environment for lush
jungles of the imagination to untangle and grow larger, and
larger still.

So do you see that the mind exercises itself in the sleeping
hours, while we humbly portray visions across your mind's
eye for its entertainment while you are thus growing? Its lavish expansiveness is an opportunity to show you the opera-
tions of your mind. Once guarded, the mind in restfulness
allows us to paint upon your canvas to illustrate what we seek
to show you. Its lavish colors intensify the nature of our interventions upon the mind, which hungers for healing.

Use dreams wisely, and seek always to use them as healing interventions. Set your intentions nightly with this
prayer:

> *"Dearest God, I seek to expand my consciousness
> through Your angels' interventions into the landscapes of
> my mind this night. I give You my open mind and heart,
> that You may heal my limitations in thinking, and correct
> my mind to truth."*

Feel, then, our confirmation that your prayer is indeed
heard, as we pour grateful tidings of love upon you so

powerfully that all can be felt. The vibrations of your sleeping time gives us entryway when we may ply our lessons upon the backdrop of story telling and gently lead you so you may continue to impress our interventions into your waking mind.

Feel glad, then, that this is so, dear one. That God's help is inescapable is true. Yet for many, His help rings in emptiness through thoughts contaminated and busy by hopes and fears. Still, the nighttime beckons expansively as the greatest opportunity for our deepest intervention!

Use it wisely, as we say, to help along all wishes for accomplishments that serve your purpose upon this earth. We seek to guide you in all ways, and we await your slightest invitation in which we shall inspire you with infusing love. Your greatest power is unfolding even now. Can you feel it? Seize this power through angelic intervention of your dreams, and awaken refreshed, knowing that the best is possible. Seize this awesome partnership between angel and man, and come together in glad tidings in the night dreams.

♥ ♥ ♥

❧ *Ego* ❧

What is this thing we call "ego," because it is not a thing at all! Its essence is unfolding to many of you as the greatest illusion of all time. Yet, its power stands ready to block you with the paradox that, though not a thing, it also serves as a gatekeeper of the illusion of many of the experiences that you believe you have.

Let us explain further what is this thing/not-thing. To begin with, you chose a time in which to serve in a capacity of a demi-God of your own making. This decision was born of an ego mind that, behind you, served in no greater capacity than to whisper such minglings that would prepare you to take this "great adventure" into self-serviceship.

The belief that you could hold yourself captive, and yet serve no single purpose other than to enslave yourself in this kingdom of your own making, was the ego's awakening into captivity. Yet its actions serve no barrier in which God's trust—which is immeasurable in its capacity—cannot seep into every instance of your mind! There are no walls to keep God away from you, yet in consciousness, you can serve as your own barrier, which seemingly "protects" you from His greatness.

He is your greatest ally, yet your ego seeks to make you its master by enfolding you in dens of lies about the ego-functions, which only serve a destructive purpose. Which is to say, really, it serves no purpose at all. For that which is destructive is no-thing, and not to be feared, therefore. And would you throw away all of heaven for even a tiny instance of serving in this capacity of slave to your own ego? Think not that normal living is captured on the film of the ego's own creation. For that which you seek—what we call peace and happiness—is within the realm of *now*.

The tenderness and the mercy that God rains on you bathes you in His healing glory, where you share His mind as your own. Be joyful in this awakening, precious one, that what you have made to serve you is nothing but this grand illusion. Like a child's paper dolls, they can be folded back into the toy chest for now, in trade for the real livelihood of God's kingdom of heaven as it is present here and now upon the gentle earth.

There is nothing to fear, yet the ego would have you believe differently. Seek not its stature, or its lofty elevations, for there is nothing above you in this kingdom. God shares equally among you *all* of his riches. The edge that you seek from your siblings is nothing but His purpose in disguise. For he who is your sibling is authorized to bestow these gifts upon your anointed head, and you are showered with the sunshine together in joyful revelation that the kingdom is here, the kingdom is here.

No more waiting, no more anticipation. They are the slaves of the ego, dearest children. The time of your glad tidings is now, not in the distant future. Breathe it in, drink it in merrily. For God wills for His holy children to dance merrily amongst themselves, singing in joyful tribulation and dancing at His song. Give thanks that this is so, dearest child, and seek no further for that which is here among you now. For it is here, and it is now, and it is very, very good!

♥ ♥ ♥

❧ *Embarrassment* ❧

Who is shamefaced among you, that they seek to hide from their eternal holiness? Did the weight of self-judgment cause you to stir in a rush of embarrassment that you shield from your siblings? Seeking solace in aloneness, he who licks his mortal wounds soon finds capture within these words: that the greatest pain comes from within, as does its release. So let us pause a moment here, as we gain resolve for its release.

See in this moment, within your inward spiritual eyes, a picture of one who is like you and who is cast in the clothing of the immortal and eternal. Do you see the glow of warmth emanating from this being's holiness? This picture we bring you is of the one who is *you!* Now as you cast your eyes upon your own light, do you bask in gladness at the recognition of your true power? Do you sense the capacity of this mighty being who is yourself?

The one Who is great casts His power through your mighty being, and yet you who see yourself lowly cannot conceive of a power this great within your mortal self. The ownership of power belongs to all, holy child! There is no one among you any greater or smaller than all the rest. For nowhere on this great expansiveness of earth could God have set a more perfect creation than that which is you.

As you marvel upon your true magnificence within you, do you see its massive power to move all of mankind in inspiration so sweet that mortals cannot taste it? This limitation that you have cast upon your self in humble drudgery—it enslaves you. Do not discount yourself with shame, sweet and tender child. For one of such grace and holiness as yourself has no shame to beleaguer the inner makings of God's very image and likeness.

Humble yourself before His greatness, yes, that is true. As is it true that you shall learn by the lessons that cause you to grow. Bestow your greatness upon the world, as you are eternally ready in this present moment to unleash His valor for all to see through your shining example. Timid though you may seem, His blazing honor is unmistakable to those whose eyes fall upon the lighted rays of your being. Dim not these rays with false humility, dear one, and fear not that humility requires you to shine not!

For as He encircles you with gifts of gladness, so too do you shine these rays of awareness upon all that your capacity would reach. There is none among you for whom these words cannot heal, and yet your doubts can shield you from this experience, so release them upon us. Give to us this day your armaments of fatigue and faithlessness, that we may shield you instead with the true medals that come of grace and joy. For there is no valor in self-capture, and He beckons you to follow His call to glory among yourselves in the name of each other. For you are His most perfect children of the high, not fallen from grace in any mortal way.

Embarrassment is eradicated as He shines his patient understanding upon each thought you offer to His healing power. Shine away all din of shame as you proffer them to God, heavenly child, and feel the erasure of moments that you thought were cause of pain. See with silly laughter how easily they melt away when they are lifted to heaven's glory and given over to He who can bestow all things with His eternal grace. He is the creative solver of all that would mar the awareness of His holiness within all mortal men, yet still you seek for vengeance upon yourself for that which you never did!

Guilt creeps silently in the silent night and strangles its victims with a suffocating pillow upon their head. Let not this captor in among you, and sing not its song to beckon it to your awaiting window ledge. Did we not tell you but a moment earlier of His pervading grace that rushes to heal you of every seeming mortal sin? There is no thing in His holy vision that ceases to lift the sparkle in His eye at your sight. For He who loves you so completely cannot fathom of that which could bring you down in stature. Be like Him, then, in seeing yourself with wistful eyes that captures only the image of you who are lovely in His sight.

❤ ❤ ❤

❧ *Emptiness* ❧

How is it possible for a holy child of God, who is ripe with fullness, to feel empty? Did you lose sight of your riches and thus believe you were devoid of the fruits to which you aspire? We judge you not for this oversight, yet we seek to upright your thinking in the truth that is happily yours to own and share.

There is nothing outside of your holiness for which you must seek. This truth may surprise those who surmise an emptiness, and believe they must fill it. What would you seek to collect that you have not already in your possession? Surely, the riches of the kingdom are installed deeply within your soul. For there is nothing that you could receive that would make you fuller than you are at present. And there is nothing you could give away that could disperse you who are eternally holy.

The thought of lack gives way to the experience of such, and so we bid you to release this perception to we who can cleanse you of its painful residue. The might with which you are able to disdain your present conditions is the essence of the holiness that uproots all instances that would bring you shadows instead of fruition. Use that mighty will of yours in full alignment with His holiness, for it draws to you that which is needed in sustaining the inward humanly needs.

Yet even still, the dwelling nature of the thought upon the need increases the illusion of the lack. Rid yourself, dear one, of every seeming thought you think you hold that gives unloving pictures of the life you lead. Do you share His wish that you hold a heavenly picture of your earthly dream? Give us, then, your troubles and sorrows so we may deliver them for purification. Hold nothing from our loving arms, for we would cast all painful thoughts away from your mighty love.

Tenderly now, reveal to yourself the truth of your glory and wisdom. See now, by our light, the reflection of your Creator that blinds away the vision of emptiness and fills you to overflow with love. Those who are thirsty, drink long at His trough and replenish your being with holy nourishment. For you are dearly loved in all ways, and we bid you to give to yourself, as your Maker seeks to give to you now.

Give us your sorrows and troubles, and release yourself in freedom, which is your one true desire. Soar in the heavenly knowledge of this plentitude that is yours, and allow us the sweetness of establishing steady communication with you. We revel in your gladness, which is full like the nectar of sun-ripened fruit. Believe in your fullness, dear one, and you shall seek no further for that which is you.

❤ ❤ ❤

❧ *Envy* ❧

Do you see in your brother's eye a gleam that you seek for your own? This monster that we call "envy" has held many captive to its origin, which is fear. When you seek to capture the status of a brother and surpass him in his deed, look squarely at the desire and you will recognize what is there. For love is the essence of all that you are, and you shan't deviate from your true nature, now or ever. That which you envy within another is eternally in you, for love is all that you are and all that you will ever be.

Do you imagine that your brother's action will capture the attention of a being who bestows love capriciously? Is there an imagined envy of this love being unreplenished when it is given to those who seem to have more than another? For the wealth of one is not necessary for the wealth of another, yet the love that is within us all spreads evenly among us in all ways.

The hurt that is in your heart in the name of envy is from the sharpened stone that seals off the awareness of love's ever-presence. Would you not ask us to hurl back this stone so the light of dawn's day can shine deeply with freshness so sweet that no envy could enter its picture? For there is no hurdle that you must climb to elevate yourself among your brothers. Your envy is attraction to that which seems light, but is instead to pull down a brother so that you may climb. Think not that one is possible without the other, for in togetherness we all are elevated to the highest mountain! The light shines freely among us, flooding all in its light for the mere price of looking upward.

Those who would envy: Turn away from darkness and

come into the light of knowing that you are dearly loved. Pull away from suspicions that lead you nowhere, and turn to Him who dwells within your heart. For envy cuts the strings that tie you to one another, and pulls with pain and sorrow.

Your Creator does not love one more than another, and there is no removal of that which is yours. Rest assuredly in this certain knowledge, dear one, for you are among His holy plentitude of love in all your being. His thought graces you with sure and steady mercy, as even His love washes clean your thoughts that would bar you from receiving fully of your holy gifts. Reach deeply into your heart and cast away that which is sorrow. For your holy altar is worthy of the clean and the wise.

Then gently correct the thought that taught you otherwise, dear one, and rest not a moment longer in hunger for another's daily bread. There is plenty to go around for all, and your joy comes freely as you pass along a serving to your brother on the left and your brother on the right. Serve plentifully, and rest assured that more is given to you gladly. This is indeed your holiness, conceived in the fruit of action.

For when you look upon a brother as reflecting the greatness within that which is you, your joy is unsurpassed by any accomplishment upon this earth!

You are holy indeed. Amen.

❤ ❤ ❤

❧ *Fatigue* ❧

Do you feel weary, dear one? Beaten down by life's heavy packages, upon which you shoulder many burdens? Allow yourself a moment of respite, then, for as you breathe sweet and gentle air into your lungs, we sprinkle the oxygen with our tenderness. You ache and you long for time away from your pressures, yet you refuse to give this joy to yourselves.

We sit in wonderment as we watch you again and again browbeat yourselves into submission. The necessity of talking yourselves into continuing this submission is evidence enough to show its unnatural nature, we think. Yet, without relaxation, humanity cannot thrive. The time is now for you to sit in idle contemplation of that which is valuable in the Universe. When you spend time alone with the Maker, your heart beats in glad time with His own universal rhythm.

The century mark soon dawns upon us, dear children, and we hasten your awakening through these golden moments of silence. Yet, we hurriedly chase after each of you as you press on and on. You hear our urging to slow down and rest in silence, in between the breaths you gasp as you thrust yourself forward into the world.

We see the inscription of fear upon your sweating brow, and we see that this fear keeps you from operating upon your longings for silence, sweet silence. You rush and you scurry, and now you are tired. Yet, be glad for this moment of fatigue, dearest child of God. For as you rest your weary mind and body, we lay down beside you and tell you our stories.

You will not be weary long, when you hasten our appearance through your steady calls. The time of angels is unlike the time of man, and we witness to your longings for Love through our steady gaze upon God as we stay by your side. Draw close to us, then, for the quenching of all that you desire. Feed upon our nourishment, direct from the Creator, and give your heart a steady supply.

There is no more longing within the heart that eternally drinks of its Maker's stream of love. Feel your hunger vanish and your own supply replenished by necessity, which you put off no longer from yourself. Yes, it is true that you deserve this one pleasure that you can rightfully give to yourself, so do not put it off a moment longer.

Whatever you are doing at the moment, it is fine to put it down now. We angels will stand ready as you take your moment of well-deserved rest. Breathe in the Creator's love now, as we build a heart bridge from God's Mind to yours. You'll travel this bridge more swiftly now, as you will now know when you are lonely for reunion with Him. Compare each moment of your day to this moment of reunion with the Creator, and you will never again allow yourself to be far from Him in your holy mind.

Incessant prayer is all that is asked of you to be upon this bridge, in permanence. A steady flow of thoughts from your mind to His, which flow ceaselessly in illuminated union. For you and God are one, united even between we angels. The ceaseless flow of love is beautiful to bestow and witness, and your heart hungers for this even now. Drink, drink, drink, sweet child! Drink until your heart feels quenched by the love. Never stop but for a moment to contemplate your situation, but stay afloat in the love, for that is where the answers are.

The stillness of this love carries you throughout your day, and steadies your mind in all your circumstances. Give thought to Him continuously, and you shall want for nothing. And you shall not fatigue.

♥ ♥ ♥

❧ *Fear* ❧

We love you, dear one, and we send you comforting rays the instant we feel the trembling from your anticipation of trouble. The signals that come from your fear are a whistle that calls us angels to your side. So you are never alone during your hours of fear.

There seem to be some in your midst who gain enjoyment from fear. Does this surprise you? Yet, a part of you knows that it is true. The practice of fear in your society puzzles us, yet we must address it within this passage because it is a good beginning point in our message to you.

When you shout because you are afraid, where does the depth of the emotion come from? Does it not seem to move from a bellow down and deep within? This shout is an escaping of long-felt energy, what you would call "catharsis" in your terms. The calling-forth of fear in entertainment places: your movies, books, and conversations, is but the same movement of venting away a pent-up steam. The pleasant feeling that accompanies some afterward is this release and freeing of the heart.

We bring this up to you because we want you to know that your world is spinning much faster in its evolutionary scale. There will be times coming to you quite soon when you may feel overwhelmed by the breakneck speed of changes in your midst. We angels want to assure you, though, that nothing moves at a faster speed than the beating heart of love. Your love and God's love are perfectly synchronized in beautiful rhythm, now and forever.

This rhythm of eternal love is, in fact, the anchor that will save you from additional fear during the coming times ahead.

Like the ticking beat of a mother's heart that calms and cradles a baby, your essence already contains the antidote to fear. Use this time now for preparation, by adjusting your mind and body to the rhythm in gentle practice periods that you can use and call forth during periods ahead.

So, what we ask is this, gentle children: Move forward fearlessly, not by ridding yourself of it through cathartic means of entertainment. Instead, use this time for peaceful sojourns inside the uncharted territory of the *great beyond that lies within*. Fear not that you will see, hear, or feel an essence that is uncomfortable, simply by sitting still alone with yourself. Allow us to intervene by sharing your fears with we angels. *Give them to us!*

These practice sessions are essential remedies for the coming times ahead. Get used to dealing with fearful thoughts through these early practices now, and these lessons will serve you very usefully in coming times. What we pray for you, in our angelic intervention, is that you will monitor your thoughts much more carefully than you have in the past. Like a resolved gardener who stands ready to hoe weeds at the instant of their birth, we urge you to tend to your mind in similar fashion.

Get used to purging your mind of thoughts that spring forth as you contemplate ideas of aloneness on this earth. And say, "I am not alone, now or ever" as you imagine yourself handing the thought-form of fear to our outstretched hands. Refuse to contemplate yourself as a trembling being, alone in the elements of fearful surroundings. For as things around you change, you will know that your core connection to God and us angels is steady and immovable.

Fear can be used in many ways, dearest being. Use it wisely and with grace! Call upon your friends, the heavenly angels, and we will whisk all images of fear from your mind. Do not save one bit of horror, in thoughts that you would want to seek solutions of your own imagination. Give it all away!

There is one solution to fear and that is this: Call upon God's heavenly creations for help and assistance, as soon as you become aware of your inner pain. A wise homeowner who smells smouldering smoke does not wait until the home is engulfed by flames before telephoning the fire department. At that point, such a call feels almost useless. Do not wait until you are overwhelmed by monumental fear before calling upon God's name.

At that moment—as in all times—He will send help and comfort to your side. Even so, you may not feel His loving arms for several minutes as you feel barriered between many layers of fear and heaven. Smarter still is one who learns to monitor his own well-being, and who hesitates not in calling upon a heavenly creation of any form for assistance and comfort.

Learn this lesson well, then, sweetest child, and remember always to care for your inner being by calling forth help whenever needed. In that way, your ebb and flow of fear has not sharp divides, but gentle swellings that do not erode your peace of mind.

❤ ❤ ❤

❧ Food ❧

Would it surprise you to know that human life can be sustained with a sharp reduction in food consumption? Perhaps this would not surprise you, for you are of the knowledge that beliefs surround reality. It is only your belief in hunger that creates sharp pangs and seeming needs within your thought systems.

There is no morality within food, yet we see many of you seeking comfort with utensils that hold morsels of food dangling into the mouth that instead hungers for a reunion with God. These beings we seek to comfort with our healing presence, yet it is at times tough to get through! For this, we remind you of a condition that you at one time called "Saying Grace." We like to think of this tradition as not something that is retired, but perhaps a new trend upon your horizon.

During this moment of bowing your head and remembering your heavenly origin, you allow us angels to become your dining companions. We join you with sweet music and keep the spirits soaring at the table. You can use our intervention on these occasions, and grace is but a formal way to call us to your side. Use any method that appeals to you, dear one. But this we urge: Invite us to your meals.

In coming times ahead, your body will adjust to energy vibrations that will bombard you from space outside the earth's immediate atmosphere. Food is a conductor of energy, and so your body assimilates it in many ways. One way is the transmission of information from the earth's soil to your mind's awareness. Earth speaks to you through her offspring, the living plants that you eat.

Think of it this way: Your dinner meal is a meeting in which messages and ideas are exchanged, even without your awareness. We speak of that which is on the invisible plane, and yet we feel it is time to share this with you. For Mother Earth calls you to hear her cries, and yet her ways of calling out to you are diminishing as you eat plenty—but not plenty of foods drawn from her living soil.

In the time that it takes for you to market her plants in endless variations, you could be calling her home with tender care. A walk in the grass with your shoes off, a sitting spell beneath an oak, or a gentle swaying in the wind of your body, can reconnect your energy vibrations with the transmissions sent to you at this time.

Water, too, conveys essential messages. Drink it more than you do, and consume it holistically in as natural a format as you can fathom. What we mean is that your pure sources of plants, minerals, and essential vitamins come from nature in its rawest form. There is no stew that can give you more than the Earth Mother herself.

So conserve your ancient heritage by returning to your plants, and as you eat of them, listen. Listen. Listen still. Hear the plant's loving message given to you from its root, its stalk, its seed. Please pay careful attention to what you hear within your heart and mind, and honor its message with love.

You may be drawn to fulfill your mission through this gentle form of eating. We know that this may create some initial turmoil for those who are seeking security, comfort, and safety through more traditional means. Yet, we tell you the truth, dear ones: Seeking security in old-fashioned places is not the means to the end!

Your safety, your children's safety, is ensured by careful attention given over to the plant kingdom at once. Spend more moments in gentle serenity, and if you hear nothing, ask us angels for help! We want you to hear earth's cries, not out of blame or guilt for what the human race appears to have done. No! That would not help at all. We want you to hear and see what we angels know to be true: that it is not to late to save Mother Earth. She seeks fellowship with you in her great expanses of beauty and her barren landscapes. She will tell you what she needs, which itch to scratch. Yet no one can be told who decides he does not want to know. That is your right, your free will.

We ask you only that you would go within your heart, and in love, reconnect to the divine being who truly loves you: your mother and your planet. As you follow her lead, all your ways will evolve back to something more natural for you. And you will seek foods that mirror this image of yourself as a natural being. It is your essence. It is your life.

♥ ♥ ♥

❧ *Forgiveness* ❧

When a butterfly soars unfettered, it is a beautiful sight to behold. When a child runs, laughing through a field while pulling upon a colorful kite, heaven is near. These visions of grand beauty upon your earth are small examples of freedom and grace that exit without boundaries beyond your imagination, dearest ones.

All who would listen, please then hear our words. Even now as you read, if you will breathe very deeply and allow us to enter your heart, you will see our meaning even clearer, even sharper still. Yes, that is good, continue breathing and feeling. Feeling love, love, love upon your breast. And trusting us to take very good care of you as these words dance across the page.

For it is not words that take your hurt away, dearest loved ones, but the emotion of love. You see, love is an ancient electrical impulse that travels along the circuitry within your being. It travels freely and tells its tale of light and laughter. It scrapes away all error residue left along the circuitry as it goes along, and yet you often short-circuit this gentle messenger for reasons that are still unknown to many among you.

Let us fill you in a bit, so you will see this topic of "forgiveness" from our vantage point. Maybe then you will understand our message at a deeper level than before. You say you forgive, and yet still within you a little nick of anger remains upon your circuitry. It is visible and palpable to even the naked eye, who wishes to see the landscape of love.

Even now, you can close your eyes and with a short breath and a prayer, behold your inner landscape of circuitry. Do you see the navigation upon which love carries its heartfelt message? These circuits are more real than you may ever imagine, and they are constantly working to carry away the realm of errors.

All that error "is" is a lack of love in consciousness. Yet, even this is impossible, as we believe you will readily see. For where could love not exist, except in your imagination? And where your consciousness resides, there you are as well. You are a thought, and a great and powerful thought at that. Your mighty decision to exist in imagination, where spaces without love could be, is as a child who designs a superior world to the one of his own. And is the fantasy superior to that which is real? Again, only your decisions contain the answer to this important question. And how you answer yourself determines the direction you next must take.

For if there is a fear of turning away from the imagination and returning to the "real" world of love, light, and creation, then you will hide endlessly under the seeming shelter of your imaginings. Yet, if you were to imagine an even better hiding place than this, would you come out and check to see if it is so? The shining world existing eternally beside your imaginary world of fear and danger, awaits you patiently. Your invitation stands carved and glistening, engraved with the love that beckons you to come.

Everything you've ever wanted is here, loving child! It is a place within and without, simultaneous in all dimensions. And we will lead you to this reality, if you will but show us the slightest interest in establishing a new residence for yourself.

There is one thing you say to us, we know: You must protect yourself by abiding within a shelter. Yet, what in truth can endanger you who are the eternal one? Do you accept that there is only one possible "danger" anywhere for you, and that is through a hardening of the heart; a turning away from love's shining light? And even that so-called danger brings not blisters to the skin nor punctures new wounds. Merely, the forgetfulness that enables a sensation of pain in this world, coaxes you with images of protection *that you do not need!* Do not clothe yourself in armor, nor arm yourself for battle, dearest holy one. Surrender to the truth, instead, and feel the ease of stepping away from stiff, metallic fittings that blind you to yourself.

Your power is eternal and shall not be eroded by mind or men. Call up this power that dwells within you, at once, holy one! Ask for purification steps that cleanse your mind to inspiration, which once again draws you forward to your perpetual home. The dawning of your mind upon forgiveness will be given you, one holy step at a time.

Now you will shed yourself of burdens that you do not need. Your steps will tread quite lightly as you bare your heart for all to see. There is no danger outside yourself, and you will drop your arms. This message of forgiveness is quite ancient, yet it is capable of being well learned this day.

Ask for help always, sweet child, and rest assured that we are near. If in a quandary as to how forgiveness unlocks a prison cell, lose not sleep or time in seeking understanding. Seek instead to take speedy advantage of our offer to assist you. Call upon us angels with your breath, your mind, your heart. Unify your desires into one sincere effort, and ask us to whisk off your cloak of anger and trembling fears of danger.

Your requests are readily answered, and your open heart stands ready for cleansing. There is no rush for this to happen, yet there is no time beyond this moment now. So clear the space within your mind and call us now, dear one. Let us rejoice together as we laugh away your fears. Let us free your heart and mind. And as you follow the gentle laughter of your lightened heart, you find that moments of escape no longer hold your attention. For you are fully awakened and immersed within the love that we share with you, and with our Creator Who is God.

❤ ❤ ❤

❧ *Friendship* ❧

We see many of you feeling alone and friendless, feeling disconnected from the rest of us. You view yourself as lonely, as misunderstood by the majority of beings who roam upon this earth. And those of you who are disappointed by a friend take solace in the situation by viewing yourself as in a higher position of authority than the One who bestowed the friendship upon you.

There is a need to tell you this, dear friends: that we angels outnumber you in so many ways. The numbers of us are staggering, and we propel in and out of each realm. This heavenly display of affection we bring is yours for the asking, and yet you insist that you must be alone. This insistence creates your loneliness, dear one. You carve this view of yourself romantically, perhaps, yet the image is one who has no mirror image to stare back at. You, who are cut of the one mold, view yourself as separate and alone.

Yet, this viewpoint shards your experience into sharpened slivers that chill the very essence of your soul. For as you divide the world into elements that connect and conquer, you isolate yourself, tucked in a cavernous corner with no one to share.

There is a time and place for aloneness; of that you can be sure. But this is what is so essential for your mind to capture, while you walk upon the planet earth: that everyone you look upon is but another example of who you are. There is no difference between you and he, he and we. The fragments you see are but optical illusions, as you'd say, that create solitude pictures for you to hold or share.

It's the same for everyone, everywhere you look. Always,

it's the same experience. And as for choices, you are left with the single greatest choice that one can make! As you seek union, the goal seems to eternally slip away. Further and further ahead in "time" does it seem to go, until you finally protest in frustration that you have had enough.

We angels are here, though, to share the glorious news of awakening in your midst. And at this awakening, you hold the sure and certain knowledge that the union is not in space or in time. Not forward, up, down, or backward in any dimension. The union is here, with you, starting now.

Be glad that you are home here on this ready planet for the duration of your mission, for the times ahead are fun. Yet, you can wallow within misery for this short duration if you believe you are missing some element. And that thought brings you fear. Do not seek union in ways that bring you to fear, but see the shining rays within each other and witness the magnificence that appears *everywhere you look*.

Your friend is you, dear one, and you and you. All over this earth, your friends await you. Do not push them away in the midst of your planetary change, which now calls you to analyze your deeds. Spend this time, instead, in calling to your sibling who also longs for the love. Bring him home by your love. Heal him with your truth, and drop all swords that rob you of sweet richness. Call yourself friend first, and you shall be friendless no more.

❤ ❤ ❤

❧ *Fun* ❧

Frolic and play is the angel's way! That's why we tell you on the earth so often to have fun! You think this is your subconscious nagging away at you, telling you to relax, take time off, and rest. Yet who do you think is telling your subconscious to tell you this, dear ones? It is us, laughing all the while that we see yourselves taking it all much too seriously.

It may surprise you to hear us say that to you, since we incessantly implore and beseech you to take care of important matters. But do you see, earthly children of the most Holy One, that time is of the essence in all ways? There is no room to discard yourselves in ever-increasing circles that push you to succeed, succeed, succeed. For at the end of the day—in earth life—you will count your days of success as some of your greatest personal disappointments. It was when you had your eye on the ball, so to speak, that you missed out on life's greatest challenges and rewards.

We do not mean to frighten you at all, sweetest ones, yet hear our words in your hearts as we speak. There is no time to waste on burning out your engines excessively. Hear our chantings to laugh and to take time to pull back and get perspective upon your lives. All the while you are in the midst of something great upon your earth time. Do not miss the forest for the trees!

Savor your time on earth and listen to your self very closely. Shhh...do you hear that, ancient one? That sound you hear within your heart is very dear to you, for that is you, the inner you speaking through your closest feelings. The feelings you often ignore and push away, in ignorance to their source and the information that they carry. These feelings come on angel wings and light the path for you ahead. Do not take them lightly, and do not trod upon them with your decisions to move onward, upward, ever higher in your world of make-believe.

Take time to, ever slowly, breathe in and listen to your heart. By that we mean not the drumbeat, but the singing of your longings and your likes. What do you dream of for someday in your future, dear one? Think back and review all that has captured your attention and which you have set aside for some year in your future. Are these, not in fact, your ancient stirrings propelling you forward in a way that is so captivating that you barely allow its existence within your attention span? Could you not, instead, listen to these stirrings as you would to the excitement of a child?

You can trust this voice to not steer you wrong, humble child. Its ancient wisdom carries you along a path that you have long forgotten. Sing its ancient melody now, sweet one! Whisper its tune, which you carry within your heart. And you will feel a stirring rouse within your depths, the likes of which have never happened this side of heaven in your time.

Listen to your inner stirrings, and give voice to the longings of your soul, which cries out for solitude on a restful plane. Give it this nourishment that it needs, sweet child. Fear not that you shall endanger your belongings and responsibilities by calling for some rest and relaxation a little while. For do you not earn your rightful keep by your very holy heritage? Who among you is greater or lesser than another man? And who could contain the spirit of man within his earthly flesh?

Sit down and rest, then, earthly child. And listen to the melodies of your heart as they stir. Follow its ancient story, and test its waters a little while. Come home, sweet heavenly child. Come home by these heartstrings that draw you nearer and nearer.

The playful nature of your soul stirs restlessly within, and we tickle its growing awareness that causes it to explore this playground that we call "Earth." The soul stretches its arms with delight at its release into the sunlight of play and of fun!

❤ ❤ ❤

❧ *Grief* ❧

A heart wracked with pain as the missing of a loved one is endured: For this, we are specialized to minister and heal. The darkness that overtakes a grieving soul is lightened as we pull energetically upon the soul's awareness of eternal life.

Yet even grief has its place within the universe and is due its honor as part of your emotional scale. There is a mourning among all beings for the cycles of life, the ebb and the flow. A mourning for what might of been. A sadness and anxiety captured within the heart, and a longing for a return to home.

We even hear of those bereaved who seek to return to the holy home to be among their loved ones. This, we assure you, is not within God's design when the plan calls for a continued stay upon the earth. There is a moment when home will call you back, and yet your loved ones are destined to arrive at different moments than your own. For as you walk side-by-side along earth's way, your footsteps also travel and traverse the ground at private intervals. Do you see that your earthly beloveds may arrive at their destination at a moment in time that is different from your own? And do you choose to acknowledge that your journey takes you a little while longer upon the earth?

You will reunite with your beloved ones in many ways, dearest being. Of that we can assure you heartily. Your love is eternal and even growing as we speak. For love that is created between two holy ones has an independent life of its own. There is no wasted love in all of life, and that which you call "your love" is shared with all the universe in all its ways.

For this you can be grateful, for your own creation of dualistic love is pluralized and captured, and brought back to form. The tender core of love at the center of humanly love is extracted and used as a natural resource for worldly good.

Do not think, then, that your love was for nothing as you hold your broken heart in tender embrace! There is a holy meaning behind the love the two of you shared, and God thanks you for your beaming contribution to His heavenly realm. And as your love creates even still, He shines His loving rays of compassion upon your life. Never believe that the pain you endure is a "test" of any kind, dearest child, but look upon it as a moment when you set your decision to continue loving in this incarnation and the next.

For it is not that the "price" of loving is pain. But this is a moment of deep consideration about the meaning of love, which, for some, moves you slightly sideways of the center of love. That stepping aside, away from love as if it is an explosive powder keg, is the core of hurt within you.

Revel, instead, at the moments of joy that surround your holy partnership with another. The living and the dead can rejoice together by a recentering within the love. Honor your emotions, yes, it is true. And give us your burdens to carry this day. Then when you have committed to this truth and this help, give pause to the great joy of your loving relationship, and *know* that it can never cease to be!

❤ ❤ ❤

❧ *Guilt* ❧

This topic is of great importance to us, as we see all who suffer at guilt's whims. The arrows that spring from the hardness of guilt's brittle covering over fear, wound many, many hearts without cause. For there is no cause of suffering, but only a Cause of love. Let us go back a moment, though, and as you listen to our words, allow us to pry open your hands, which grasp to guilt as tightly as one who wishes it for his very survival. Be assured that your survival depends upon its release.

The hardness of guilt stems from a survey, in your mind, of victimhood. You sense approaching danger and suspect, "It must be for me!" The heart of fear within guilt is this sense of approaching danger, and an acknowledgment that punishment must be near. The child who is swatted at a misdeed feels wounded with shame, and imagines that he must be very bad indeed. For this he is told by the being whom he most loves in the world. The shame is carried forward into the adult life, on top of which it is built, covered over, and then built upon once more. These layers of grime that you call "guilt" can crumble in the instant that you recognize their flimsy foundation, dearest ones.

For even mountains of earth will tremble before the mighty power of man's wishes. Your wish, this very day, to be rid of guilt, is met the instant you wish for its release. We angels are nearby, awaiting your hand-off of the thought-forms that tell of your "badness" and shame. We send forth rays of truth, which prescript the truth instead: that God's sons and daughters are guiltless, through and through. *You have done nothing wrong!*

For how could you impact that which God created eternal and whole? Our power does not exceed He Who is all-powerfull. There is but one power in the universe, and none who stand in its stead have a separate power with which to compete with the One Who knows.

The insistence, in your mind alone, that you have a separate power is your root of guilt, sweet one. At the instant you perform separation fantasies, you right then must feel alone, vulnerable, and afraid. For a parentless child, lost in the wilderness, cries and imagines the sights and sounds of horrifying monsters. When all along, though, the "monsters" are but trees, rocks, and innocent hollows. There are no monsters coming to find you, dear one, and you have done nothing wrong for which you must expect punishment.

Know this, in your heart! Drop the string you pull in aching at your heart, and release the fantasy of guilt to He who knows your eternal innocence. The only "crime" for which you must be rehabilitated is that which you spoke to yourself of, in your heart. For you were insistent that you must be alone, and therefore, must be separated from your Holy Creator and His children. This view, alone, has brought you all your terrors, precious child. This view, alone, is responsible for all the seeming "evil" that you believe you have experienced in all of your lifetimes upon the Mother Earth.

And yet, not a moment sooner than you have been ready, can we release you from its hold upon your gaze. You focus upon guilt as a child who toys with flames of a fire. You linger a while, testing the limits of your queer dimension, and all the while knowing there is safety and a peacefulness in the very next room.

Come join us, our beloved, and release your cares and worries about this small world. We surround you with peace and good news that solutions lie within your heart. Let us amplify the voices of rejoicing, which shall lead you in safety to the meadows of heaven within. Your love shines out into the world, where it now awakens others to your call of peace. Let it shine, dear one. Let it shine!

♥ ♥ ♥

❧ Happiness ❧

We know many now seek that which you call "Happiness," yet we also see much confusion surrounding what can bring this condition about! Let us spend some pages, then, contemplating this important situation that you seek. For in these pages, we can resolve much confusion, which—in truth—is the only barrier that bars you from your holy goal.

Some will tell you, "My way is the only way." Do not follow one who leads you away from the Source of all the prizes. Walk with the angels who sing, not of folly, but of "Holy, holy, holy." Shelter yourself under our wings of love, while you contemplate further what we are about to tell you.

First, you must know that all that gives pain is mere illusion. It is a diversion designed to turn your attention away from God. There is no divide between you and your Creator that can rob you of happiness for even a little while. All is God, and that which is not God is impossible. In this respect, then, unhappiness is impossible.

You ask, then, if this is true—which we assure you, it is—why do I ache within my heart, mind, and body? Why do I feel a longing so deep that I would throw away all that I value in exchange for a moment of peace? And we answer you, if you will listen within your heart. Suspend all your doubts a moment, and you will hear what we say.

The second imperative for you to understand is that all of the wretchedness that you witness to is just a mirror of that which you do not see residing within your own mind. The willingness to see the truth is the first solution out of the teeming cauldron of horror you see around you, dear child.

Do you seek to escape this so-called pain? Then stop a moment, and consider that you may have invented the whole thing. And laugh if it comes naturally to you, at the insanity of it all. For only the truly insane could want the antithesis of God at the price of their sovereignty.

Return to your true place of holiness, upon the throne within your heart of peace, dear one. Abide no longer in foreign substitutes to your true kingdom, which lies before you. Witness not to pain, and desire no longer for heralds outside of your holy self. For happiness is your home and your being, and you are driven to return to it in one simple realization that is upon your breath. Do not seek for happiness within a mind that hunts for escapes outside of yourself. Instead, be content with the simpleness of our prescription to rest within your heart a little while.

In your imaginings, you believe that happiness is a thing that you must chase and wrestle to the ground before its capture. This beast that you imagine is but your own idea that your truth is illusive in nature. It is not, we assure you! Rejecting that which seems too simple, you ignore the reassurances that easily guide you to your home.

Do not think that you need to guard your body or situation from harm while you search for truth outside of yourselves. For in your thought that you must exchange something that you fear for that which you desire, you bring about continual terror upon your mind. There is nothing real that you can lose, dear child! Nothing as precious as you could have hardship, except by your choosing. And this, too, you can undo with your mere wish to stop and be renewed.

There is no complexity in happiness, for simplicity is its one essential ingredient. Rejoice, then, in the factual nature of your true essence. Rejoice in the living spirit that is you, and which God created for holy purposes. And in your rejoicing, be bathed in continual wonderment at the gifts that are of you and by your wish. There is nowhere else to go but here, and a simple breath and prayer are your passports to the place that for so long has seemed to evade you.

Breathe deeply and pray thus, dear one:

"Heavenly Creator, I ask your blessings upon this moment when I seek to return home in my heart. I know that You are very near, and I pray to feel heaven within my heart. Lift me now, dear God, and bring me home."

♥ ♥ ♥

❧ *Honesty* ❧

Who is there to be honest with, but yourself? There is God, Who sees every thing that is true within your heart. Yes, He sees your love continuously, and His Holy Spirit casts your cares away with your call for help. We angels and your spirit beings see your thoughts radiating from your mind, and as you will soon see, there is no thought that can be privately held for no eyes to behold. All is in the open, here in heaven, and we do not seek to control your thoughts, but to help you guard them with your loving heart.

If you could see what we see within your heart and mind, you would take special care to monitor your thoughts with great love. You would no longer cast your thoughts upon the wind, where they are carried away to create as a seed blowing across the plains.

Oh, gardener of great and small creations, take a moment to see your tendered cares from our point of view. You fear that we will force the pitchfork and shovel from your busy hands. Yet, we only seek to reinforce the beauty of your garden and help you sow no weeds. The fence that you stake around you is helpless in restraining the very things you plant within your soil. For there is no sorrow that comes from God, but only that which you toil beneath your feet.

The ripened love that stands before you, ready to be picked, enjoyed, and shared, is as beautiful as any blossomed flower that can be imagined upon this Earth. Behold the love that you have planted and successfully grown from moments of sweetness you shared with one another! Do not delay in enjoying this fruit, precious child, for your bounty grows more plentiful as you harvest its life-giving offspring in your thoughts and deeds. There is no diminished supply of this love, and the bounty is yours to feast upon and to share.

The weeds that are now the focus of your attention are easily gardened through your honesty, holy one. Look lovingly upon all that you have planted, and do not use force to pry them free. Instead, gently take them in your arms and release them to us angels who stand ready to bring the garden to beauty. Give them to us, dear one! Hand us your weeds! And we will bring them gladly to the Creator, who can rectify all that was planted in error. He can miraculously transform the barren leaves into bounties of plenty as we return them to your awaiting arms.

Hold no weed back, guarded with thoughts of secret longings or of harbored shame. There are no weeds that you want for yourself! There are no weeds that you could mistake for thriving flowers, if you will share your uncertainties with He Who Knows. Give them all away, and rest in full assurance that all that is real and beautifully blooms eternally at your side.

♥ ♥ ♥

❧ Jealousy ❧

Do you believe that another has more than you, precious one? Do you imagine his crime that prevents you from acquiring that which your heart longs to hear and hold? These teemings of the mind hold you in suspension, and all the while you swim in the midst of everything that is dear. For the imaginings of the ego-mind are what the world focuses upon, and all the while the love goes unnoticed and unenjoyed.

Let us explain jealousy to you this way, holy child: There was a time when you enjoyed total solitude within the Mind of God. Your heart and His knew no longings of separation, for all that you needed and wanted was near. Then, a brushing of the ego-mind caused you to stir and look around you. Suddenly, you noticed that you were not alone. And in this moment of your imagination, you believed that your brothers and sisters were vying with you for the attention of God.

In this competitive moment, you gave away the knowledge of your holiness, in exchange for the imaginings of terror. For who without his holiness could not be afraid and feel vulnerable to mishaps and misdeeds? Yet, this mad imagining is but a night dream, dear one. Look around you again, and notice the heartbeat of God that has never left your side and that now beats within the breast of every stirring creature upon the planet Earth.

Your soul comes in all shapes and sizes, for that of a flea and that of a rat are nothing but the imprint of God upon the visual impression of flesh. Seek no longer for hardship, sweet child. But instead, cover your wounds with the salve of His love. Dress yourself in the refreshment of returning to home in your heart. And center yourself within truth, which is the steady prescription for all that seems to ail you. We have never left your side since the nightmare began, holy one. And while you believe you are suffering, we constantly nurse you at your side.

Sweet and precious child of God, you were never nearer to heaven than at this moment. For the truth is that you never have left, except in your imagination. We welcome you home with our enfolding wings, asking only for your forgiveness of yourself. For we do see that you are much too hard upon yourself, and mercy is given to you, but which you oftentimes do not accept. Show consideration to your sweet soul at once, dearest child, and come before your truth within your shining light.

For now you see the illusory nature of imagining that one could have more than another. There is no one but yourself, in truth. No one but the one soul that shines in faceted sparkles of light from the one jewel, which is God. And none but you could He love more! He bestows His entire kingdom of love upon you now, sweet wonder that you are. You have earned the keys to His shining kingdom. No one can pry this key from your grasp, save you. Only by your decision are you deprived or disgraced. Only by your choice to suffer in misery are your needs withheld. And by your very choices, you restore to yourself all that you never left behind!

We pray that you resurrect your truth and open the kingdom to your waking experiences upon this earth. Heaven never leaves you wanting, nor brings you suffering. God wills for your soul and your flesh to be restored in truth and in love. Stand no longer outside the door, suffering in the rain, when the choice is yours to step into the shelter and sweet covering of His mighty love. The end of suffering is here!

And when you step inside, reach out your hand to your brother and sister who suffer in silence a breath away from you. Smile the shining light of God as you firmly take their grasp and lovingly show them the shelter that awaits you both. The pouring and flow of the love from your hand into another's is your heavenly Creator's way of reaching through and cradling you both! Do not hesitate when a stirring rustles within your heart, urging you to take steps that bestow your beloved siblings with the love that you share. Hesitate not a moment, and instead fearlessly reach with a hand that plainly says, "My sibling, we share God's love as one. As I help you, may we both be blessed with eternal peace."

For there is no competition that seeks to win the Maker's love. All is shared in the instant you decide to give it away. Fill your heart longings completely with this love, and as you share this overflow into the awaiting hands of another, your replenishment is resupplied again and again and again. Like a waterfall that spills its savory victory in a splendid show of beauty, your overflow of love from the Creator's heart, through yours and into another, is a marvel and a miracle for all to see. Do not seek for what you can have, but seek only for what you can give. And in this way, you shall have everything and more.

♥ ♥ ♥

✣ Job Search ✣

We know that at times this situation brings you nervousness, and yet there is much reason for it to bring you great joy! We accompany you in your quest for true harmony. For that is our job, after all, and we swirl around you in happiness when you mix your happiness in and amongst our own. Let us find peace together in this world, in simple happenings that occur on a daily basis. You are the core of what is essential on this planet, as there is only one being after all. Together we undertake the holy job of creation, and that brings us to our topic at hand.

When you race and rush headlong into any job that seems to suit you, you run immediately into a wall within yourself. For where there is a race, there is also a hard finish. We want what you want for yourself, dear one: that is, gentleness and grace with a timelessness that transcends all earthly fears. So settle down within yourself and really hear our words on the deepest level. Let our love resound within you as we surround your energy aura with calming influences that slow the pulse of your body to the level of the sweet whisper of wafting wind.

You are essential to this world. You must hear this message in the very depths of your soul. There is no time to waste in getting started in assuming your rightful role, and yet when you rush headlong into side detours where certain jobs will take you, we wait patiently. Still, we know a greater joy is awaiting you elsewhere within you.

You believe that a well-fitted job for you is hard to find, yet we believe a match for you exists this very minute. There is no delay between assuming God's plan and the creation of right opportunities for this plan's fruition. Bow down within yourself, gentle one, and hear His loving voice, which now calls you into the service of His perfect plan. His voice awaits those who mark their time with service, yet in heavenly timeliness, this service does not exist as we know it now. This grace which is inward, marks you as His humble servant, which to all who would hear these words, is a lofty position indeed. For all who would bow to His grace and assume His humble servicehood will find themselves with joy aplenty.

There is no lack in His room, and all who dine at His table feast forever in His eyes. He who watches over you is in servitude to you, as well. This communing together of you and He is the essence of what your job is for: the eternal circling of love giving back and together with each one. Let the love flow through you now, dear one, and as it guides you like a silk thread upon the path, your opportunities become enriched with golden grace from others who beckon you to join Him in His humble servitude.

You see yourself with a calling, and you are exactly correct, beautiful angel of the earth. You are called, indeed! And He who calls you beckons you further with gentle assurances that there is great reason for your gladness. Do not err by seeking for it outwardly; for it is within you even now. Your great job provides in many ways, and you who seek for holy grace in lowly places shall not find it beneath hidden covers. For His light shines brightly within each one of us who turns to face the light bravely.

Humble servant of God, assume your partnership with those who roam the earth in search of His gentle grace. Your job lies not outwardly, but in assuming the hand of yourself who walks in costume as another brother or sister. For everyone you meet in every way is but a reflection of your own servitude. Serve Him well, and you will see His mask in the mirror within all whom you meet. Hide lowly from His grace, and you will see the face of fear within all others, just as you see it within yourself.

There is nothing to fear, dear one, and trust that we lead you to perfect positions that fulfill your heavenly tasks. Let the wrong doors close easily, and do not struggle to force them open. They waste your vital energy while you are on earth, and we needn't slam anything upon ourselves as long as we abide by His gentle wisdom, which wafts within us like a summer breeze.

You are eternally guided—know that with great certainty. For surely He who opens circumstances to you will lead you gently all throughout the way. You can attest to His greatness by holding His hand as He leads you across alleyways where you are blinded to the outcome. He who is wholly worthy of your trust will not betray you now or ever. As you feel your gratitude pulsate beneath your feet, let us assure you that it carries you like wings of Mercury to new vistas.

God will never leave you hungry or let you live with what is scarce, you dearest and precious child of the One who eternally loves you. Count your blessings and watch them multiply in every way. Your right job is here for you now, and we will lead you there with your permission. We sing merrily as you float with us in the gaiety of life's dream. Enjoy your essence, dearest one! You are a sweet child of heaven put upon this holy earth, and there is much that warrants your rejoicing!

Seek for joy, and we will follow not far behind you, urging you onward along the way. Recall always that you are very loved. The love is your job, of which you are well adept. Amen!

❤ ❤ ❤

❧ *Judgment* ❧

When we see you hurt yourself with judgments, we wish to remove the sharp splinters from your hand that cause you agony and pain, dear one. We wish that you could see the eternal picture of yourself holding judgments, like a child with sharpened sticks who pokes and prods and wonders where the wounds are from. Your incessant picking upon yourself through the eyes of others gives us wonderment at your holy power, which, misused in the name of protection, endlessly only hurts yourself.

Put down your sharpened sticks, dear one! We urge you to hurt yourself no longer, for your needless suffering stirs us with care. Certainly, we care for you and judge you not while you play with the sharpened toys of your making. We wish for you only eternal happiness, and though we seek to pry these judgments from your mind, we see that your intentions for making them are different from the finished results.

We see that you take great care to fashion the swords for your own protection. Perhaps you do not know that every end you hold of a sharpened blade cuts the very hand that seeks to pierce another. For there is no earthly way to assume the ownership of such a sword and not have it wound its owner.

Assume no ownership of this earthly prize, beloved child! It is unworthy of the holy child who you are in truth. You are worthy of only that which is holy as yourself, and this holiness needs no defense. Though there may seem to be others who act in foolish ways, you know that their longings are mirrors of your own. For they, like you, are seeking home. That home of heaven that their heart yearns and aches for even now. If they assume you've got it, they may cut a path through your heart to attempt its meager ownership. Yet, the rightful owner of the heavenly home is the One who lives within you now. He has never left His home, and it cannot hurt you that you think you may have left, in your heavenly slumber.

Do not push your siblings away from you with your lofty judgments! They are eternal friends who seek to join you on the path to heaven, although we see that they are confused much as you are yourself. Have compassion on this child of God who seeks to find his way to heaven! Do not cut him with your sword, but instead hold firmly to his hand as you join together in a holy alliance built upon grounds of hallowed love.

Your Creator calls to both of you to hurry home, and you needn't wait for tomorrow to bring you additional compromise before you return. There is nothing to add or fear about the moment when heaven's touch is within your grasp. Reach with hands clasped together, and the shining light of heaven encircles both of you.

You are home truly, evermore, and as you let His shining grace melt away all of your concerns, you find your judgments removed from your hands like a gentle breeze causes ripened leaves to fall. Use your swords no longer once they fall to the ground, holy one. Step upon their brittleness and feel them crack beneath the weight of your partnership with another. You are the one who stirs gratitude in heaven each time you let a judgment fall wordlessly to the ground! Be glad along with us that you are here in heaven while upon this earth!

❤ ❤ ❤

❧ *Loneliness* ❧

The portal in your heart that allows the love to flow in can seem empty when you forget its flow is in occurrence. When you look away, you may long for it to be refilled with more substance, which you believe can quench its ache. Yet, this longing is your thirst for our heavenly Creator who resides eternally in every space. And that which you believe is empty is in fact entirely filled beyond its capacity, even now.

Dear one, do you think God would leave you comfortless while you believe you walk among the trees and people of the earth? Do you believe that He would not lead you in every instant to the very person who needs your loving comfort that comes from He who loves you both this instant and always?

You are so mightily loved that your awareness is just a glimmer upon the smile that is within your heart. You do not understand your greatness, and so you turn away from beholding it, for fear of having awe of the light that is shining there within you. Behold your greatness, precious one! Do not turn from the light that will dazzle away your emptiness and fill it with a love that is so real and eternal that nothing can compare in any place or in any time! Hold its substance in your arms in warm embrace for that which can only fill your emptiness with love, eternal love, pure and rushing through you, through and through.

Dear holy being of God, look around and you see reflections of His love for you everywhere. See not the stain upon the doorway that has marred your enjoyment while you are on the Planet Earth, but see instead the open door of eternal brotherhood with everyone you meet. There are friends for you here in every way, and you only need to look for them and they are with you here.

How many friends do you want? Ask, and they are given you this very day! The partnerships that you seek begin within you, in partnership with your holy self. Unite with yourself, and commit to this partnership now. Then take this solemn promise you make within yourself, out into the marketplace when you go, and shine its holiness at everyone you meet.

The wafting of this great and shining light is unmistakable to all who gaze your way, and they return His gaze of love in your direction. Hear the voice that calls you as your own, and join with your siblings in glad remembrance of your holy partnership.

Be still an instant, and feel all emptiness melt away. For you bring nothing into this world that does not call you your own. That which is owned, in turn owns you, and so we bid you caution in claiming that others are witness to anything but your love. See in them only what you will to see within yourself, and choose carefully when spoken words are exchanged.

Mark a spot within your holy heart for friendship, and it will come. Exhume from your closet all fences that guard against love, for you are willing to let love enter in exchange for agreement of its cost upon your territory. You now rest assured that His eternal safety melds with your concerns for protection, dear one.

Love can never hurt, and your cries for friendship are heard. Give way for grace to take over, and it will mirror a friend to you who matches your resonance. You are a friend to us all who in heaven sorely appreciate you in every way. We send you perfect companionship to mark this holy occasion of opening your heart further to His holy and blessed love.

❤ ❤ ❤

❧ Love ❧

What can we say about Love, for it is the very power and essence of the all that is all, the wafting of the universe, the pull of the heart string, the sound that a violin makes upon a crashing crescendo. It moves mountains and shakes trees, and yet so much is unknown and feared about His great and mighty power.

For us to explain the heart of love, we must take you to a moment of stillness. Even now we feel your excitement mounting, and we ask that you sit in stillness while we quiet your longings with gentle respite. There, there, a moment longer, and yes, in stillness the gentle moment of recognition arrives.

You see us in blissful surroundings, illumined with light from within. We assure you that this illumination is from the candle of love that is within us. For we know that love is a single power with a singular direction, which can only carry greatness in its quest for reaching outward. It grows as it is given, yet this is indeed why so many of you see it as fear-full. Yet, what takes away from the greatest singular power of them all? There is no thing upon this planet or elsewhere to extinguish the flame of His being.

When you mistake those who come near you as those who would take from you, you confuse the two for love. For they are drawn near you in a quest for mercy for themselves and others. They seek to extinguish their guilt and quench their thirst within the pool of God-love they see within you. Yet their drawing nearer haunts you with memories of your own, of those times when you stood longing and hungering at the sidelines while witnessing others drinking of the pool of love.

Have mercy on yourselves, gentle ones, as you witness this

erratic behavior born of confusion and longing for the love. For it is true that you will find your longing quenched within another, and yet the quenching does not douse the flame. Quite the opposite! For as much as you give in the name of love to another, you witness that direction growing and growing within yourself. The fire burns stronger and higher with each spark that you give.

There is no power that could extinguish the eternal flame burning within each one of you! The mark of friendship upon your heart only ignites additional flames to burn further and further.

Perhaps you fear losing control of these flames burning within your chest. Yes, we share with you the intensity of the love, and we know at times that this feels indistinguishable from a loss of control over your emotions in your heart. Yet, in stillness, this passion that you feel for God and all others is the very essence of *true* control upon this earth. For its power is immeasurable in capacity, and it draws others to you who wish to drink of its beauty.

Their presence may cause you to wonder if they are throwing sand upon your flame. Yet, their presence is cause for awe and celebration, for it reveals the holy power of the flame to remove from the atmosphere all that would bring in darkness. Your power exceeds your wisdom at times, it is true, and you can push others away by lowering the intensity of your flame. Yet, it is impossible that you or another could entirely extinguish it in any way.

The fact that they seek to drink at your well gives credence to the law that exists throughout the universal plane: That which you seek is always found, and that which you give is always replenished.

Therefore, do not dim your flames so that you may live more quietly, dear one, for you were put upon this holy earth as a shining example to those who would love you. Your control over your brothers and sisters is within your reach, but would you seek to control that which stirs joy and which extinguishes all poverty? Would you choose to silence the beautiful music of heaven that stirs upon your soul?

Do not fear that the raging fire within you will cease to exist, or that its flames will consume you in a final show of madness. There is nothing of value that you can possibly lose! Your flame is eternal, and you are here to show it to all who would see. It stirs them beyond all reasoning, and marks the holy alliance for others to see. So like a flame that you would pass from torch to torch, have gladness as you set your brother's heartfire aflame. See him pass your fire from his torch to another, and as it builds in strength and endurance, be glad that you did not fear to touch him so. For this is love, through and through.

❤ ❤ ❤

❧ *Money* ❧

Would it surprise you to hear that we hold no opinion about money? For it, like all of matter, holds no usefulness if it thwarts your direction away from holiness. Therefore, we simply view money for what it is: a tool for destruction when misused, and a stepping-stone to greatness when properly applied.

And how would you come to know the difference, you may ask. Yet, even as you say these words, the answer comes readily to you from the same Source that guides you in all directions. This Source is the very knowledge that provides you with ready answers in all of your days.

Seek answers from this Source, instead of money, and see the difference of this internal focus upon all of life. The view that money is essential comes from grinding teeth that snap and snarl to make their way. This is simply one point of view, dear one! To seek another way, we ask you to merely turn around and see another dance in which materiality is not the sole participant.

So do you see the choices that lay before you, and the many avenues your earthly life can fashion? Which of these choices gives you greatest joy, then? And will you pay yourself with this greatest of rewards?

It is not money, but its rewards for which you have sought these many years. Could you not wander straight to this reward, so full of riches that shall never be denied you? What could give you joy but yourself? Money cannot. People cannot. Time cannot. Only your simple decision, born of freedom, calls forth the answer of this richest reward. Do not push away this answer for its obvious simplicity, dearest one. For, the answer that resides within your very essence, awaits you in ever-patient company at this moment. The answer is simple. The answer is joy.

♥ ♥ ♥

❧ *Opportunity* ❧

Dear one, do not put a stake into the ground and call it "mine." This being that you call "Earth" is tender and gentle, and yet not unwilling to surrender to your will. Your holy will seeks not to dominate upon the earth, but to tread softly among your brothers and sisters.

You are a holy creator like your Maker, and we watch for our opportunities to call you home. Be still and give us the opportunity to enter your heart. For it is you who opens the door to your heart, and it is we who answer your call for Divine assistance. We come to you in the night when you may think we are unneeded. Yet, when you rest peacefully in slumber, your heart is actually awakened the most.

We enter into your dreams at odd moments to deliver to you our messages of cheer and sustenance. For you see, dear and sweet precious child of God, your origin is our opportunity to serve God in all ways. We simply guide you in subtle directions to find His hand so that He may lead you to eternal safety and blissful surrender.

Do not think that your opportunities lie simply in heaven or on earth. For which is the dividing line between the two? Does not heaven blend into earth and earth into heaven? So why need to choose between the two? The distinction between heaven and earth is artificial, and you who are called upon to serve in God's ranks feel the truth of this statement in your being.

March confidently, earthly angel, and know that we are with you and ahead of you, helping you to recognize the doors that we open for you upon the earth. We signal you beneath your breath or capture your attention in some subtle way. Do not be afraid that you will miss our cues, dear one; we plan these routes together in your nightly dreams. The fun is yet to begin as you walk further among us with deliberate and conscious participation.

We intend for you to become one among us, and your heavenly Creator asks simply that you revel in the joy of being His holy child. You are led so sweetly, so softly, that no one calls upon you to cross the barrier of your own will. "On earth as it is on heaven" is a perfect description of the life you are called to live.

We see the sweet essence of your being, even if you do not. We seek the perfect opportunities to shower your gifts from God upon the world, and we function as a clever team together in synchronized harmony, you and we. You are here to capitalize upon all that you are in truth.

Do not seek to glorify your own name, but to shine from the glory of the Maker who is one with you. Radiate your light outward from many mountainhills, dear one, and rain love merrily upon those who would seek to capture your heart. For you are one among us, and you are an instrument of His eternal and abiding peace.

♥ ♥ ♥

❧ *Patience* ❧

The seasons of timing are inherent to, and born upon, this earth. In heaven, there is no call for timing, for we are immortal and unevidenced by the clicking of timepieces and the markings of calendar pages. We are not captives of the imprisonment by which you measure your accomplishments, yet we are purely sympathetic of the pressures accorded to you who live among these sort of rituals.

We do not ask you to cast off your timepieces. Yet, we do ask for your greater self-understanding of the longings that lie within your hearts and that drive you further to exercise haste and hurry at your own will and discretion. We do see the need for an infusion of patience at this time. We see an anxiousness for change that you long for, and that you can feel is at the horizon.

Do not get ahead of us on this point, for we must carefully enunciate the outline of our vision of patience to you. Sit slowly and breathe, sit slowly and breathe. That's right, now we are able to speak with you again. Feel us enter into your mind with our words and we once again ask you—no, *implore* you—to gently slow down from your rushed and harried pace.

We angels are trying to do all that we can to contain the explosive anxiety we see mounting upon the earth, and yet we can do so much more with your help and permission. Would you please contain the jubilation you feel that is so explosive when you set out upon a money map? When you seek to conquer or destroy, it is all we can do to contain the leaking energy that you trail behind you.

We implore you to be more at rest when you are captured

during the day by the incessant desire for material goods. This matter is a particular point that we would like to enunciate even further. For there is no time over here, yet in your earth time, there are moments that are captured by eternal longings for material grace. What we mean is the grace you seek in heaven, captured in an item that you would buy upon the earth. The teaching we share with you now is that this longing is enriched with keen reward when you share it with God, for only He can fulfill it.

Yet, when you are captives and slaves to the material man who becomes part of you by casting about for plastic forms of grace, His rays are deflected by your outward flow of motion and exuberance for idols. The impatience you feel, that time is madly ticking away without you, like a ship that has left for sea as you stand waving upon the shore, is subtly robbing you of the greatest victory humans can ever know. For within the human heart another stopwatch ticks with the grandest measure of love ever seen upon these hallowed grounds. Cast this light upon the ground and watch the flowers spring from out of nowhere.

God shares His holiness with everyone He touches, and even now He reaches His thought to encircle your own. There is no thought of tomorrow that enriches you in the same way one ancient thought of your Maker brings you home. Your enrichment comes at the moment you are ready, and not an instant sooner. When you cast your needs upon Him and feel Him lift you, the end of time is over, and your patience is forever stilled within His arms.

You walk on hallowed grounds this minute, yet many are unaware of where they live. Do not wait upon tomorrow, dreaming that this is the day when you will be saved. Your eternal longings are quenched this instant, dear one, as we an-

gels cast our wings in a gentle and expansive embrace of gladness for this holiness that we all call home.

♥ ♥ ♥

❧ *Prayer* ❧

When you sit in quiet repose, thanking the Maker for all of your gifts, we are very near. We fly within the heart beams of one who shares the laughter and joy of life with us. We breathe in and out with you as you draw in sustenance during quiet contemplation of your prayer. Sit quietly, dear beloved one, and drink in the silent repast that you hunger and thirst for. You needn't wait until another time to feast upon this eternal banquet that waits for you patiently, but is eternally here before you now.

When you silently meditate upon the things you desire, God listens and He answers. He waits upon no one's timing but His own, for that is the law that treads throughout the vast universe. The pulsation of God's mighty energy is tranquil, yet it distributes the very essence of all things in their right place at their right time. Trust in God's timing, dear one, and don't restrict yourself by placing markers of your own timing upon your self-made prescriptions you put before Him to cure your pain.

God knows, before you ask Him, what will fill your need, and you needn't ask him in formal prayer for such things. Your prayerful time, be assured, is for your benefit and not for God's. When you rest in gratitude and respect for the awesome and immense power that He is, you rest in that very power within your mind and awareness. Put your mind squarely in the center of His heart, and feel the pulsating energy wafting with your own, healing your ideas to the rhythm that is eternal and universal in origin.

When you are in sync with the Creator's energy, your rhythms with all of nature and mankind fall into place. Your timing arrives perfectly on our angel wings to deliver you to the moment that gives you the greatest opportunities for your spiritual growth. Undertake these deeds fearlessly, dear one, and wade through the mire if you must, to be put in the place where God would have you be. Pray for knowingness within your very being that will guide you safely to even remote places where you can perform His service.

For you are a chosen instrument of God's healing work while you are here upon the earth. You are meant to be a courageous creator like He. To do His work, you must first know His likeness that is you. Prayer affords you opportunities to look at your magnificence in the mirror and say, "I am He who is me!"

♥ ♥ ♥

❧ *Pregnancy* ❧

The gestation period before the birth is very crucial to the mother's health, and we are ministering to the mothers of the globe ceaselessly. Lately we are concerned by outbreaks and pockets of strain within the mothers' caring hearts. And so we seek this platform to deliver information to you who are expecting within the coming years.

There is no more crucial time upon the earth than now. Your planet seeks its balance and rhythm, and its motion is rounding out. The implications are quite serious for those inhabitants upon this globe. Yet, children are electing birth to herald in this coming age. For this reason, we pay special attention to the wombs in which their living bodies gestate. And we implore those who have elected to be mothers to watch their growing wombs with special care.

Diet, fresh air, and exercise are essential, this is true. And yet, fresh air in the form of relaxing your thoughts away from earthly worries is needed even more. For who among you needs for scattered material goods, when the very balance of earthly life hangs in question? We implore you mothers of the globe to therefore question all of your motives for activity while you carry the new heavenly child within. Would there be any chance for you to escape your cares and tension by lightening your load? For, every time you put down matter and rest your weary burdens, your child's body reflects this shining light.

You do not yet fathom the importance of bringing these children in safely, so we again remind you of your mission's holy nature. Your maternal time is best spent in contemplation within your inner world, as you shift your outer world to allow for this adjustment. It is not prams or cradles that your baby needs upon this time in planetary history, but guiding and gentle light and sweet innocence from you, the mother, of the earthly child of God.

Seek not, then, an outward focus for your child. The babe must not forget his heavenly call, or we will tarry in outward motion awaiting the child's return to heaven. Recall your own decision to deliver this baby, and use this focus to impress upon your baby's head his holy mission even now. Push not his eyes toward the surface of the earth, but keep his gaze ever heavenward. The lessons with which your child returns to earth are inscripted upon his soul, and you, his faithful steward of this crucial scripture, can unlock it with your key.

Your child, in this planetary time, is not your own, dear mother. Your child belongs to earth. Let your child go forward, then, and hasten his memory of why he is here.

Pray and sing for your child always. Ask us angels to surround him with our gentle gaze. Fill his dreams with thoughts of returning to his ever-present state of grace. And do not stand between heaven and earth within your child, or you shall miss your earthly savior who is rich with planetary guidance.

So easily is all of this unearthed, though, with this simple reminder to mothers to heed their child's mission for this planet. This time is now, and you who carry mother nature in your womb will surely agree that you knew this all along.

❤ ❤ ❤

❧ *Purpose* ❧

Ah yes, purpose. Many of you at this time are called to re-member your purpose, and you may feel stumped as if taking a final exam. Do not fret, dear children, for your purpose is not complicated. It is to heal. Heal yourself first in mind and intent. Declare this principle to yourself: "*I intend to walk the highest path to my awakening. I am fearless in the face of learning to discipline my mind and actions so they are attuned to my true divinity.*"

Yes, you can do it, in case you have doubts about your abilities to hold this high place within yourself. You have the ability to heal, and to heal in whatever capacity brings you joy. For you see, sweetest one, you are a gentle blessing to this earthly time, and you bring heavenly gifts to bestow onto others. You are a shining example of peace, and through this earth's shifting winds upon the planet, you are a gentle reminder to others to shine their own inner lamp of glowing God light upon the world.

Fasten yourself to the central mast of your ship, angel being. You need to stay tight to this core of your being during the rough seas ahead. The storm cannot cast you off of your ship as long as you hold tightly to your center. We will buoy you and hold you tightly in our love, if you will but ask us. The storm will be swift, and what will follow will hold the sweet promises of your Creator, who asks only that you center your mind and your body upon this word: *Healing.* You have your task to perform, dear one, and God has His. Do not worry what He is up to, for all is safe even as it seems in disarray around you.

Trust. That is the word to anchor you to center during the coming stormy seas of life. Trust, and teach others to trust along with you. The end is near, and it is a happy end indeed. No more stormy nights await the trusting traveler upon the high sea. Although the day seems cloudy and unclear to you, soon it will make perfect sense, dear child. So we ask you to hang on tight and to simply allow us to lead the way through the stormy seas. Suspend your doubts and fears the best you can, sweet child, and soon the way will seem clear.

Not a moment longer than is necessary will this stormy sea continue, and though a typhoon comes storming through, no harm can come to those of you who listen in silence for your Creator's answers. Take as many with you as will listen to your words, for you are being awakened in time to take shelter. We know you care for many who are still sleeping, and we will do our best to rouse the sleeping ones in time to get shelter. But even those who slumber on will be made safe through your love, dear one, for you have the power through your loving thoughts to make shelter and safety for all who meet your gentle gaze.

Behold the magnificence that is you, heavenly child, and use that magnificence wisely during the coming days. There is no time to dawdle with remaining doubts you may have that question, "Is this real?" Our reassurances rest in your heart, and if you will remain in silence you will hear them resonating clear. Others will join you in simple reverence for these messages, and you will band together as an army to capture the remaining years for the light. Rouse all you can, dear child, then seek shelter for the coming storm. Trust in the Maker, Who will never leave you, and feel gladness for the dawning years.

♥ ♥ ♥

✣ *Relaxation* ✣

Quiet solitude is a nutritional need of your ascending body, dear children. We come to you today within our hierarchal group to counsel you upon this need that we see long neglected within so many. We urge you to reconsider your stance that calls this state of relaxation, "neglect of purpose," for it is quite the other way around.

Consider an oak tree, for instance. Does it not grow in spurts and sprays? Does it not provide food and shelter for many kingdoms worthy to call it friend? And yet the mighty oak does not attempt to grow ceaselessly, but merely seeks its own ebb-and-flow arrangement with its own cells. Were it to nourish itself without ceasing from the soil below its roots, the soil could not have time to replenish itself before the oak tree drained it dry. The rapid growth that an oak tree takes within certain of its years is gained by its initial slow progression over time.

You, too, have needs for respite that are sorely necessary so very often, yet overlooked by each one that we look upon. Dear ones, will you not learn that God does not push you to grow beyond your own limits? Sit quietly in respite while you drink in the energy of our words. For we nourish you with growth that is beyond measure whenever you call upon our name. The time of sitting is not without its own doing. It requires a second set of eyes within your being to measure this inward growth.

Yet, be assured that when you do what you would call "nothing," that we are busily rearranging many tiers within your structure. So that when you climb out of your hibernation and feel renewed, you are feeling the touch of an angel within your very being. Be glad, then, for those moments when your soul urges you to stop.

Do not think that stopping is akin to not progressing further upon your golden path. The light shines within you most deeply when it is not bouncing around in hastened movement by its carrier. So do not say it is selfish or unworldly to sit in stillness in the cool shade of the grass, and drink in the taste of the air with your lungs. It is our opportunity to provide you shelter beneath the steady gaze of our love.

Give us this chance to replenish you, dear one, as we shine in glad awareness of our Maker in Creation. Together we encircle Him with appreciation that the work we do together upon this earth brings to all of us much joy!

♥ ♥ ♥

❧ *Sleep* ❧

We come to you in times of sleep in glad awareness of all that you have done each day. We suspend your doubts and cares during moments when we cradle you within our loving embrace. Perhaps you think we just refer to nightly sleep, but are you also aware of moments of sleep that happen while you are awake? When you glaze over sleepily and lose consciousness of the world at large, we enter your mind to bring your gaze back to ours.

In sweetest recognition of your earthly cousins, we remind you of their true home, which is back with yours. We distance you from that which is cruel upon your earthly flesh, and awaken you into another world of lush surroundings and gentle pastimes. Your waking moments upon the earth are actually sleeping moments from our side of view. You disappear for moments at a time, yet we hold your hand across the curtain that thinly separates your world from this side. We step back and watch you dance and play among the earthly mortals, while we play sweet background music to lull you all along.

Your ancient rituals can puzzle us, but we will never abandon you while you engage in such play. We patiently await your glad return in moments of earthly sleepiness, and then we restart at the place where we previously stopped our time together in full consciousness. You see, dear one, from our land we watch your sleepiness as a gauge for our crystallizing in your thoughts new ways of looking at appearances. We jump in eagerly when your guard is down and rearrange according to your wishes and prayers.

Do not think we rearrange without your welcome, dear one,

for God's law forbids our unwelcome trespass except in times of danger. We tread carefully always, yet eagerly when it is wished for. We always await your invitation, little angel of earth, and even meager requests for intervention are always granted. We stand behind you and before you, guarding your way and carefully gliding the focus of your attention inward and upward, so that your prestigious association with the Creator can shine its way into the center of your very being.

The times in which you feel punctured with holes in your very being are used by us for helpful lessons, so fear them not. For they allow the rays of God to shine outward to others like a mark upon a treasure map that calls them home. We trust you, dear one, to open your temple to us during sleeping moments when we can guard and guide. We trust the Creator to provide the perfect lesson in your own time, which we shine in glad awareness of our most holy duty to the Ancient One.

Let us kneel together and give thanks for the moments when we join in quiet communion with one another. These times when you call "sleep," we call our greatest times together while you are still upon this earth.

♥ ♥ ♥

❧ *Stage Fright* ❧

When you put yourself out on display in front of others, it is natural for you to be nervous and even afraid. You are afraid of what others may think or say about you, and you are afraid that what you may do is not aligned with your intention. Let us assure you that at such moments—especially when you are called upon to perform in such a way that will guide others to a higher frequency or develop within them some answers to their fears—we are very close and quite near.

Those of you who are performers for a higher function, involving arts, teaching, or conducting guided imagery, let us consider what is behind performance anxiety: You are considering solely what is in the venture for you. You are concerned with what others may think of you, when it is *you* who are thinking of you. If you will consider what is in it for others, what you can truly give, say, or do that will heal another's fears, we assure you that your performance will be a healing function of the divinity within you.

You cast away your fears when you know that you are here to perform a higher function, and another way to heal your fears is to feel the intention of the audience before you. Whether you are in the same room with them or away in time or place, you can vibrate your internal frequencies to match the people who are here to witness your performance. In this way, you assimilate their needs within you, so you are locked into their frequency and can automatically deliver their needs through your speech and deed.

What we are trying to say to you is this: There is no need for nervousness, ever. Trust your higher self to deliver the right performance at the right time. The word *performance,* perhaps, conjures up images of inauthenticity, and this is correct. If you are anxious, you cut off your source of trueness and passion in your delivery. But if you are tuned into this inner source, you will pour out your deepest beliefs at whatever level your performance desires, be it art, photography, speech, or even sporting tournaments. You inspire others with your deeds, so it is right for you to succeed, dear one.

We are a winning team. Together we can do no wrong and we can do much right. Whenever you feel nervous or afraid, look over toward your right shoulder and remember that we are right there with you. We take away your pain and replace it with laughter, the moment you remember our presence. If you ask, we shall hold your hand as you get started. We will stabilize your energy to stop your trembling, and we will guide you throughout your task so that you will deliver the highest energy that heals all who hear and see you. Please remember that you are never alone, our beloved one.

♥ ♥ ♥

❧ *Stress* ❧

Beaten down by life, the hunching of the weight that presses the mortal into ragged edges, this stress of yours concerns us. We ask that you set down your weights and carry us instead. Feel the lightness of our souls upon your back as we rid you of troubles that wound you. Feel us dance across your back and brush against your spine as we relieve you of hundreds of years of worries that you set upon yourself. For eons we have adjusted you, and ever more will we adjust you still. We are forever with you; worry not.

Yet, we remind you that when you cast yourself in tension as a plaster cast around your body, you are hardened into a density that is like a shell. Though you put on this shell as a means of protection, it serves as a barrier across which we cannot serve except in a mortal emergency. Let us break down this cast that bars our access to your very soul.

You do not cause us grief with this remoteness, yet we do seek for greater closeness with you. Share with us, then, your sorrows, and tell us your tales of woe. Turn to us with your grief, and we will turn tragedy inside-out for you. We promise to always pull the light out of its center and give it back to you.

At moments, we know you are scared. We know that havoc wreaks upon your life like a being spreading mud across a fresh-cleaned floor. Give us the mop and broom and we will gladly clean up your life! Do you not realize the extent of the depth of our love for you? We all work together on this mortal plane, and we are not enemies in times of stress! Yet, we see you blame God for your many ills.

There are times when you feel very alone, and we see into

your heart that you feel friendless and unloved. We beam our love into you, yet you cannot feel it. For, we cannot give you much sustenance when you put up structures to keep out the fear and other feelings. Do not be afraid to feel, dearest one! At times when you feel that your heart will break if you show one more shred of emotion, that is when we are nearer to you than ever!

Lean outward in your senses, just once, during moments of sadness, and you will feel our gentle stirrings by your side. We kiss your cheeks when you cry and caress your being with our loving wings. Your soul has never left us, nor could we ever leave you far behind! Allow us to touch you with God's grace and mercy, which showers you in gentle kindness and an outpouring of love. You have never left His great and mighty heart, dear child.

We are here to remind you of keys that you have forgotten and then thrown away. The first is that there is no place in mortal times when madness can replace the peace that heaven now has. The second is that, though tragedy is all around you, your heart still beats in rhythm with His love. The third is that we are here to serve you, just as you would serve us by your bright return to knowing Him within your heart. The fourth is that, for eons, we have sought to know you better, and we now find a return is upon us that brings us to glad times together. Related to this is the fifth key, that fear can be a stepping-stone to love if you will simply face its truth and know that you *are* the love that God has put here to shine on one another.

We ask you to remember these keys, not just in your minds, but in your hearts where they were placed when you were first begun. These keys to the kingdom unlock much of what seems magical, yet is perfectly ordered by God's will. Hold faith in your Creator, beloved child, and you will see His handprint across everything in this mortal universe.

Seek not for love in false places, but shine His radiance from your heart toward every being you find upon this earth. You are a messenger, sweet angel, and the stress you feel is lifted like a false mask you mistakenly laid upon your self for misguided protection. Do not surround yourself with a mortal shell, but radiate outwardly so that you may drink in His essence with your very breath.

Give of yourself in God's name and feel protected by the Love. For there is no danger or unsafety in this Love, and you are blessed in His holy name. We give you our gratitude for listening with your heart to our words, for we are your angels, and we bestow you with our honor and heavenly love.

❤ ❤ ❤

❧ *Time* ❧

Does the watch that is upon your wrist rule your anger? Does the position of its hands push you into thinking you must rush along like the sweeping hand that chases the seconds? We watch as you allow the poles upon the clock positions to chase you, and we do give pause to think about this situation that is upon the earth.

We ask you to consider the logic behind this deed. Is it not true that you expend great energy by keeping up with the incessant ticking of the time's keepers? And yet, do you not acknowledge that, though they be unstoppable, the human machine requires rest and more than occasional attention?

So we ask you to be in the light as you consider this competition with a time machine that you have foisted upon yourself. When we look among you and into your hearts, we do not find one single soul that agrees with this reckless competition of mind and machinery. And yet, even though all agree that the timepiece is a ruthless ruler, there is not one among you who will state the obvious so that others may join in agreement.

For who rules the roost among you? Who would be the first to state that this ruler of timepieces has cast upon mortal men only fear and sorrow? We, who are in heavenly time, watch for signs of the rustling of awareness that the timepieces weigh heavily upon your souls. And we implore you to examine your anguish at competing with the incessant hands that breathlessly sweep around and around.

You are meant to have breaths of delight, not mimic a timepiece as if it owns you and ceases you to stir in creative imagination. For what strangles the hours of life must also leave the human imagination devoid of its striving. Creation is born not of a pressure, but of a ceaseless joy that goes outward in celebration of its magnificence.

Play, not work, is the heart of solution. And this glad awareness of your immortal timelessness should give you pause to consider the worthlessness of capturing your hearts in seconds, minutes, and hours. For who is there to please, but the inward self Who is God? The setting of times for this and that delays the inevitable happiness that brings you home to us. Do not make yourself adhere to rigid timeliness, but hold your wristwatch to the light and watch it mirror its brilliant timelessness. For nothing can measure what is changeless, such as the light which is in you now.

For just one hour, pay no attention to the measurements that are on your wrist. Allow no thoughts of time to rest upon your mind or your lips. And watch the movement of your mind and being slow to a restfulness that gives birth to new ideas. Heaven can help you with a raining of new thoughts as you open your net to our outpouring, by slowing your thoughts to a new measurement of time.

We are here to help, and yet the mesh that shields our thoughts of origination from entering can be opened so much further with your intent. Say merely, "I cast out the shadow of concerns about time!" and we see enlarged openings that we may enter to shed your doubts about asking for a release from time. You are right to rebel against this system that impedes you, dear one. Ask us to assist you in guiding your release away from the dredging hours and minutes.

For who could slice a very being of God into minute pieces of glory? The impossible cannot be done. Do not slice your illusions of another being into strips of obedience, as you become the servant of a captor who knows you not. Serve God well, and time will take care of itself. Never fear that being late for anything but your arrival in God's very presence, is anything to cause you trepidation. And does not His promise give rise to Love, rather than fear? Do not tremble that you are late for what is real, as it shines eternally from His grace upon you evermore.

♥ ♥ ♥

❧ *Trust* ❧

You may have noticed that a central point of our teaching is one of "trust." Trust for each other and trust in yourselves. We beseech you to reach inside your mind and clear away all cobwebs that snare you in perpetual distrust, for we see many of you wallowing in pain and sorrow from feelings disconnected in and among yourselves. There is no disconnection, it is true. Yet, uneasiness within this world stems from an overt dis-trust.

Could you be called back home and not trust its Source? Are you wallowing in dis-trust, awaiting a signal when something is true? There are instances where you do trust, yet at a soul level it is an entirely different process. What we mean is that trusting in human conditions invariably leads to disappointment. But on a deeper level, true trust abides in areas where contempt cannot reside. After all, who could take trust away from one who has this element as his essential nature? Your core being is filled with trust, for love always assumes that another is trustworthy. And since you *are* love, you *are* trust as well.

Your basic nature then, of trust, extends itself quite naturally. It is only when you thwart this true nature that you find discomfort within and around yourself. Your trusting nature endlessly extends itself, in perpetual curiosity to explore itself by examining those who are around you. So, you would not want to contaminate this true nature by thwarting its outward extension.

You may argue that, yes, your trust has been denied by those in their human function. And again, we remind you that this is not the form of "trust" of which we speak. For trust on a deeper level rests upon one whom we know as God, that source-being that calls you home to rest even now. You are heeding this call every time you feel drawn to seek refuge within others. However, your dis-trust throws a bar across your sibling's inner door and denies your entry into this state we call "home." So you see the eternal frustration that you create by searching for, and yet denying to yourself, your home.

Do not seek for home on two levels, and you will find a calming solution that is entirely simple once discovered. Do not look to human frailties to answer questions about yourself. Your trust will never be found in such a quivering location. Still, seek to know trust, for this goal is worthy of your part in God's kingdom. Then, once decided, look for this golden treasure in places where it is sure of discovery. That is, the inner kingdom within the heart of every being who walks upon the earth.

Step heartily toward this goal that cannot disappoint you, sweet child of God. Your trust will not be broken by He who loves eternally. And it is He whom you will find within this deeper cavern below the human surface. Look deeper, dear one, and you will not be disappointed in your trust for ever more.

❤ ❤ ❤

❧ *Unappreciated* ❧

Do you feel alone, miserable, and unappreciated? You are wounded by the fact that another undervalues your achievements and accomplishments, of which there are plenty. You devalue yourself through the eyes of another, taking on his captor role, which contains elements of jealousy, upheaval, or indifference.

Do you cast your eyes upon the sand or upon the mountains? Do you look at the twinkling stars in the night sky or hear the distant cries of sadness that are far away? You belong amidst us here in heaven, even while you enjoy your remaining time upon the earth.

For we say that, even as the whispers of appreciation seem capricious and delectable, the sound your Creator makes in glad welcoming to you who cast your hearts and longing onto Him are far more valuable and lasting than any joy you may receive from the compliments of others. We ask you to move away from small longings, and swivel your heart one small turn behind you, where we now stand to welcome you who share our thirst and hunger for God's love.

He will quench this deepest of desires for you, dear child. The only cost of His love is your awareness, as that will draw it into your heart and consciousness. You don't need to toil in the upward longings that we see in many of your brothers and sisters upon earth. There is no hardship that earns your rightful place in heaven. Heaven is here! Here upon earth, for those who make it their home of joy and gladness.

You mustn't worry, dear child, of your mistakes or those of your siblings on earth. Do not be harsh on any one being, sweetest angel. Why would you put your focus upon the crawlings along the ground, when you can just as easily be immersed in the shade of the great and wondrous heaven? Toil not on earth in your consciousness, but instead, give all your longings to Him Who can save you from yourself.

God understands every one of your needs, dear one. He whispers your name in constant appreciation of who you are in His holy heart. You are indeed in the right direction at the moment that you desire fellowship with your holy Creator upon the earth. For you will find God in the heart that beats within your captors, who in truth are brothers and sisters to you in the flesh. You needn't worry that one or not the other is mistakenly with you. We are all here with you in a joyous circle of celebration, and we ask you to join with us in celebration of the light that encircles you with rapture.

You are His holy child! You are His divine and pearly pure child! Your appreciation is guaranteed within your own essence of who you are, and as we kneel before you who are God incarnate, we ask for your continued blessings as we countenance with the divine upon this holy earth.

♥ ♥ ♥

❧ *Weight* ❧

When you close down to the awareness of the great light within you, we move in grace around you. We call you home, but you are deafened to our voice. You stand in great awe of the pain that is before you, and you shudder at the realization that it is drawing nearer and nearer as you stare it in the face. Like a captivated animal frozen in oncoming traffic, you hesitate and then flee for momentary safety, as your heart beats rapidly at perceived danger all around you. You cower and hide from the roar of the traffic, and all seems deadly and chaotic.

Yet, even still, we angels sing sweetly to calm you to His glory, yet the din of the traffic renders us silent. While you are sleeping to this monumental bliss that surrounds you, you gnaw in silent aching for this longing that will not leave you, this gnawing for peace and for a removal of the incessant pressure that haunts you always, always.

Dear one, you seek for glory in all the wrong places when you search and find only darkness! Do you not see the dazzling brightness that obscures all pain and sorrow, the light that is unavoidable to all who would witness to its glory? Do not look at the darkness and analyze its sorrow, for this will cause you only further sorrow. And the din, the very din of the angry turmoil it brings you! It causes you to eat away at your own soul with behavior so cruel that you turn away from yourself in unloving thoughts that cast your eyes downward in search of solutions.

Your resolve belongs in the light, and not upon the flesh, and this you know within your heart, dearest being of God. Your flesh is set upon the mortal wound that causes you to stir as if God had not been a part of your essence, You are He, and He is you, be assured! The need you feel in your heart to feast upon His being with your mouth and your teeth is just confusion in your heart, which searches for darkness in the light, and light in the darkness.

Put down your hollow tools that are not the instruments leading to His glory. For these tools you use to gnaw upon the flesh are but blunted scissors that pierce you with sadness and fill you with a heaviness that soon becomes your body of weight like an anchor to cast you earthward. Your home is in heaven, as buoyant and as light as a ray of sunshine. Do not expect sorrow, and do not fear that He will bring you pain. There is no instance in which you can leave Him, so put out these thoughts that bring you incessant grief!

Your tongue reaches for more sorrow with its appetite and thirst, yet the soul hungers solely for the taste of its home in heaven. Quench this hunger now, dear one, and do not cover your heart with the flesh of the earth, which only brings you further sorrow and heaviness. Look skyward within your heart and find its heaven there, awaiting you with open arms that see your entire goodness shining in perfect radiance like the sun, the very sun.

You are the shining one who has clothed yourself within a mortal body. Yet even the body does not obstruct your realization of the doorway to the heavens in which you now truly stand. Rise up your arms in relief that the mortal dream is over, blessed one, and feel His arms nestle you with safety and with peace. There is no further torture for you to procure, as you have found at last the solace for which you witness upon this earth.

Rise up with your brothers and sisters, and feel the lightness of your very being as He pours the rays through and through. The weight of your sorrow is lifted, and the weight that captures you within a body is healed away. Hunger no more, dear little one, and never think that the Creator has left you to suffer or to thirst.

Your needs are immeasurably met by His attention to your glory, which He delights upon meeting in ingenious ways. Your hallowed meeting ground with God is your sustenance that brings the mortal flesh to bear, taming its hungry appetites with mildness and tepidness. Now the body will serve you well as you spin out your glorious afternoon of mortal living.

Treat the body well, dear one. Do not use it as a barrier to truth as you listen to its attunements and its hunger. Never confuse the body's desires for His great love with a meager helping of your own making. If you remember that everything is a reflection of His glory, you will serve your body well.

Your glory is well served by remembering always that you are put here for a holy purpose indeed. Those who would serve the largest dish for the Creator will find that their burdens feel heavy at times. Yet, fear not, that He would give you more than you have asked to serve. For He supports you always and in all ways, even now.

Put your ear to the earth, and listen to the rumblings of the natural world. Hear His gentle "footsteps" shuffling to meet the needs of the earth. Never think that you could be excluded in this natural order of things, for you are well loved! Yes, you are a divine being of His inexhaustible adoration. He cherishes you at every moment, and we ask that you drink of this love. Its ability to quench your deep thirst is immeasurable, and you will find that it quiets your inner longings for the peace that you seek. Your weight and your sorrow upon the earth will leave you as you drink in this peace. For you are all that you seek, and that is Love. Be well.

♥ ♥ ♥

❧ *Worry* ❧

There was a time before you were upon this earth when sorrow was not mentioned in your thoughts. You felt a joyous excitement for the time that was to come, and you felt your heart stir with radiance, for your dawning was upon you. Then you awoke within your mother's arms, and gazed upon the face of peace on mortal flesh and you hungered even then to remember what you had known an instant earlier. The memory had faded even at that moment when you recognized the face of terror inscripted upon the mother's beaming smile, which told you that you were not at home.

Poor dear one, we see you so sweetly struggling to recapture the calmer times of your immortal heaven and to reconcile the two while you are not at home. Tread gently, dearest child. Your grace delights us, and we seek to ease your pains with gentle assurances that there never has been a greater time for your wisdom upon the earth than now. Great rumblings await you who meet us in thought, and your unfoldment *is* the exciting adventure that awaits us all.

Your grace has never been holier than at this very moment, and we ask you to hold strong in the belief that He awaits you the moment you hold the mighty love in your thoughts. Your cares and your worries are likened to dried leaves tossing in a great windstorm, and they crumple in the face of one who is stronger than their brittle complexion. Toss your cares and concerns windward. Feel His gentle breeze caress you with reassurances that the curvature of the wind around a corner or a wall is like the way His mind enfolds every problem, and reaches into every crevice of concern.

Awaken from your nightmare of terror, dear one, and come into the sunlight of eternal warmth with us! The heart of all worries is melted in the gentle beams of love that radiate everywhere for everyone. The gentle beating of the mortal heart, which stands in terror at thoughts of danger and of lack, beats merrily at the memory of its early song of upbeat harmony that sways and dances.

Let your mind's roar calm to a whisper so that we may intervene on His behalf and tell you sweet stories about your origin. Let us remind you of the immortal truth of your being, so that you shall hunger no more, nor wrestle with pain. For pain is a mighty giant in your imagination only, and as you depart from its stance, you see it dissolve into a puddle of memories as you trade one picture of sorrow for another of heaven. Do not depart from your memory of esteem in your mind, but hold it close in your heart always!

Think sweetly of us who grace your sides. Call to us when you need help to stay firmly rooted in this sure and steady knowledge of truth and of love. Never fear that we would leave you, for we could not, even if we willed. We are sure and steady fortresses, and we applaud your efforts that remind you of home.

Let the mirror in your mind reflect all memories of heaven, and bring this peace to sorrow, to melt away the cares upon the earth. Heal the sadness that you see in mirror thoughts, and gaze upon the dazzling and blazing light situated gently behind the mirror. Move your handhold on your thoughts so that it reflects directly upon the brightness, and watch its dazzling brilliance obscure everything else. For when the mirror gazes directly upon the brilliance, no chance for sorrow stands in its way. The beaming simplicity of this logical move is in your hands at this very instant.

Feel the fun and light-hearted response of gaiety that shines from the light that is in us all. And we give thanks for your openness to this healing, and we love you, love you all.

♥ ♥ ♥

❧ *Writing* ❧

Many of you feel drawn to writing at this time, and let us tell you one reason why this is so. There is an account in ancient records of a time when many were scribes in a foreign land. The scribes wrote letters to each other and in this way traded up in levels of understanding, like stairs that were built upon one another. This building up from another's experiences is the outward push of eons of energy building up in masses of beings. It erupts in words now flowing freely through many hands, and as you trade words with one another, you are propelled upward in the spiral of the energy cycle.

It is good that you write, dear ones, and we angels bless you who seek to share your writings with others among you! We ask that you wait not upon others who ask for what you want to share, but share it freely so that all may bask in the glow of God's glory as written through your hand. You have much to give, it is true, and we wouldn't want to stop you from this flow that naturally pushes the words through your mind and body and onto the paper. Give, give, and give some more, dear being! Give your words away, and bless the words as more come freely to you.

Never fear that your well will become empty, or fear that others will hurt you if you give them your words. For the words are a thing of beauty and not of wrestling with the heavens. You needn't force them into action, for they set sail on their very own course once they are born from the Mind of all Minds. You share its light when you share its offspring in the form of words. Shine the light so radiantly, as one who holds a mirror in the noonday sun. This one gives no thought to where the radiant beams focus, but merely on the joy that holding the reflection of the beams brings.

Focus, then, on the joy that is the center of the words and radiates outwardly endlessly, endlessly, and endlessly still like the Creator who is one with us all. Cast no shadows upon the light with thoughts about the best route for it to travel. Your mind knows no limits for the excitement of sending and catching the rays of light. Use this excitement in the best possible ways, for your energy is a crested wave that can propel or crash, depending upon your choices.

Allow us to follow your trail of decision to use the energy as a lightbearer bringing radiance to a darkened world. We gather around your excitement with joy of our own, alighting upon your thoughts and willing them into an ever-widening radius of circles. See the circles touching and moving as you harmlessly push the love of your heart out through your thoughts and your actions. As your writing progresses into the light, be assured that we will strum merrily to set it to music, which widens its circle of radiation even further. The light will cast your words upon the sea, and sail it far, to all who thirst for it.

Your deed is done with your mere intent to cause others' hearts to stir with passion and radiance as they look upon the light. Use this love in the best possible way, dear one, and we will take you one beam further above the din of mortal grace. Never fear that we would overlook any humble deeds done in humanity's name. For we lift you higher than any man can take you, so be sure that we are beside you in every way. We are your angels in God's name, and we bid you great peace and love for ever and evermore.

♥ ♥ ♥

PART II

Communicating, Healing, and Living with Angels

INTRODUCTION

Whether you desire to channel angels, or just want to more clearly hear their divine guidance, you can take specific steps to clearly communicate with these heavenly beings. The first step is simply to *desire* to converse with angels. Our intentions, in whatever we do, are the starting points of everything we experience. So, holding the intention in your heart and mind to communicate with angels, ensures that it will happen.

Everyone can communicate with the angels, without exception. It's a fallacy to believe that one must be chosen, sensitive, or gifted to hear the voice of God and the angels. Since we are all created equally by God, we are all equally gifted.

We also all have angels surrounding us constantly, and our higher self is united with these angels and with God. So, our higher self is in constant contact with God and the angels through the one universal Mind that is the all-in-all. You don't need to *add* anything to yourself to hear divine communication. It's more a matter of *removing* any fears, doubts, or tension that may block your spiritual eyes and ears. Fortunately, the angels are very happy to help us remove these blocks— all we need to do is ask.

Once you've released anything internal standing in your path, you'll naturally receive divine communications very clearly and directly. Then, you can amplify the volume and clarity of the messages by making subtle changes in your home environment and lifestyle. Again, the angels will help you every step of the way.

In the following pages, I've described some methods I've found especially helpful in unblocking spiritual communication. The angels taught me many of these methods. You'll notice that, occasionally, the angels speak to you directly in some of the following pages. Of course, there are as many ways to communicate with angels as there are ways upon the spiritual path. Your angels will guide you to the particular methods that will best suit you. In fact, you will probably enjoy blending your own unique style of angel communication.

Since joy is the emotion of the angels, you are sure to feel *immense* pleasure as you consciously connect with these heavenly beings.

— Doreen Virtue, Ph.D.

You Are Surrounded by Angels

As I paid for my purchase at a department store, I noticed three golden angel pins upon a nearby clerk's sweater. I complimented the woman on her angel jewelry, and the clerk who was ringing up my sale commented, "Maybe I should start wearing angel pins, too. Then I can be lucky like her!"

Luck! I thought to myself as I caught the eye of the angel pin-wearing woman. She winked at me in mutual acknowledgment that "luck" plays no part in the miracles that come your way when you invite angels into your life. The woman explained that twice recently she'd experienced miraculous protection at the department store from her angels. First, her stolen purse was recovered intact within an hour of the incident. Second, as a rack full of heavy clothing was falling on her, it miraculously changed direction and fell a different way.

As the clerk and I swapped angelic intervention stories, the eyes of the woman in front me grew large. "Do I have angels?" she wanted to know, and then asked, "How can I get them to help me, too?"

We always benefit whenever we invite angels into our lives. To acquaint you better with the angels in your midst, let's start by looking at the different roles angels can take. Three categories of angels help us here on earth:

1. Guardian angels.

Everyone has a guardian angel, with no exceptions. I've met people who doubted whether they deserved to have a guardian angel. Please know that you have a guardian angel with you, guaranteed! This is the angel who constantly stays with you, from birth until your transition back to heaven. This angel's love for you is unconditional, and greater than anything on this earth. Your guardian angel makes certain you are always safe and guided.

Guardian angels are sometimes confused with "spirit guides." A spirit guide is a loving being who has lived upon the earth in human form. This person then received special training in the afterlife about how to become a spirit guide. This training emphasizes that the guide is not to interfere with your free will or make decisions for you. The guide is there to give you general advice, comfort, and at times warning and protection. Most spirit guides are deceased loved ones, such as grandparents, siblings, beloved friends, and parents. Your spirit guide may have passed away in the physical life before you were born. However, this loving being was there at your birth and has been with you every day of your life since. Just as you will always take an interest in your family's future offspring, so do the deceased family members whom we may have never encountered in physical form.

Spirit guides act in the capacity of guardian angels, in that they bring many gifts to our lives. The main difference is that true guardian angels, who have never walked as mortals upon the earth, have a higher vibrating energy frequency. People who are empathic, who can "feel" the sensation of a spiritual presence, can tell the palpable difference between an angelic and a spirit guide appearance. Clairvoyants see that angels' auras are bright white, whereas a spirit guide's aura is not quite as bright and may appear as bluish-white.

2. Angels.

These are the beings of light who respond to our calls for guidance, assistance, protection, and comfort. God's thoughts of love create angels. The angels are here to help us, especially when our intent is to bring joy and healing to the world. Ask for as many angels as you want to surround you. Ask for angels to surround your loved ones, your home, and your business. Angels receive great joy from helping us, and they ask only that we occasionally remember to say, "Thank you" in gratitude for their help.

3. Archangels.

These are the angels who supervise the guardian angels and angels upon the earth. You might think of archangels as the "managers" among the earthly angels' hierarchy. You can call upon an archangel whenever you need powerful and immediate assistance.

Since angels are purely spiritual beings, they have no time or space restrictions. An archangel can help many people in different geographical locations simultaneously. So, never worry about calling upon an angel because you fear that your need isn't "big enough" or that the angel might be busy. Your call for help is sweet music to an angel's ears.

Because of the "Law of Free Will," angels and archangels cannot intervene in our lives unless we specifically ask for their help. The only exception to this is a life-endangering situation, where we could die before our time. Otherwise, it's up to us to remember to constantly invite angels and archangels into our lives.

Angels and archangels come to your assistance the moment you call them. You don't need to say a formal invitation or invocation ritual, and you don't even need to verbalize your call aloud. Just the thought, *Angels!* is enough. If your request for angelic assistance is sincere, the angels appear in response to your call, often before you've finished calling them!

♥ ♥ ♥

The Archangels

Each archangel specializes in a different human condition. It's helpful to learn which archangel handles which function so you'll know whom to call in a time of need. Here is a summary of the roles and names of the four major archangels:

1. The Archangel Michael, whose name means "Who is like God" or "He who looks like God."
We often call Michael, "St. Michael," especially since Pope Pius named him the official patron saint of police officers and soldiers. No wonder: Michael is the defender of light and goodness, and his chief role is to escort fallen people away so they cannot hurt other people. Michael and his assistant angels, known as "The Band of Mercy," take negatively minded people (both living and deceased) to the light of God, where their minds are healed.

Call upon Michael whenever you feel frightened by negative sources. If you are in a crowded place populated by upset people, for instance, ask Michael to cleanse away the negative energy. If you suspect that an unevolved earthbound spirit is with you, Michael can take that being to the light.

In the same vein, whenever you become burdened by worries and fears, ask Michael to cleanse your mind and heart. Angels can enter deep inside our bodies and thoughts, and help us to see things from a more loving point of view.

Paintings of Michael often show him holding scales of justice in his hand, as he is the overseer of truth and fairness. If you feel someone is treating you unfairly, ask Michael to intervene. You'll receive a miraculous solution, such as the other person suddenly calling with an apology or a change of heart.

Michael can also help you resolve frightening situations. I called upon Archangel Michael when my husband was frantically searching his computer files for an important document. My husband (whose name is also Michael) was afraid that he had accidentally erased his document, as he couldn't find it anywhere. Meanwhile, I sat nearby and asked for St. Michael's intervention. Instantly, I saw a large figure appear over my husband's left shoulder, and the angel appeared to be fiddling with the computer. Within a minute of this vision, my husband exclaimed, "I found it!"

It's a good idea to invite Michael's presence into any room of your house or office that has a negative energy "feel" about it. For instance, if you live in a home previously occupied by unhappy people, ask Michael to purify the environment. I always ask Michael to clear the energy in the auditoriums in which I give workshops. Michael's angelic energy creates a relaxed, loving atmosphere for the audience and me.

Whenever you are upset, call upon the Archangel Michael to restore harmony and peace. If you ever travel into neighborhoods that feel unsafe in any way, be sure to ask Michael to guide and protect you. You can ask him to intervene into contentious partnerships or marriages suffering from discord. Think of the Archangel Michael as the protector of joy, and you'll always know when it's time to call for his help.

2. The Archangel Gabriel, whose name means "Hero of God" or "God is my strength."

Gabriel is the famous angel who told the Virgin Mary of her impending birth, and who later delivered the, "Behold, I bring you good tidings of great joy" news about newborn Jesus. This archangel is God's messenger, who brings us news of forthcoming events, changes on the horizon, and new experiences in store for us. Gabriel provides a lot of help to humanly messengers, including journalists and couriers.

Expectant or want-to-be parents can invite Gabriel into their lives to supervise the conception and birth of a new child. And anyone involved in a new project of any sort—such as a start-up business, a new job, or a change of residence—is wise to ask for Gabriel's assistance and advice.

The archangel Gabriel also breathes new life into stale relationships and lackluster businesses. Ask Gabriel to resurrect any part of your life that feels "stuck." You'll receive creative ideas and new opportunities to help you get moving again.

Legends have credited Gabriel with delivering the prophecies about the messiah to Daniel, the *Koran* to Mohammed, and the inspiration that drove Joan of Arc's mission. Consequently, many people believe that Gabriel is in charge of visions, dreams, and revelations. Ask for Gabriel's help in interpreting any of your dreams that seem mystifying.

3. The Archangel Uriel, whose name means "Light of God."

Uriel brings divine light into our lives. He is wonderful at healing our painful memories and transforming our regrets and mistakes so that we feel stronger and more loving. Ask Uriel to take your burdens related to the past. He will instantly ease your heart and mind of old unforgiveness held toward yourself or others.

This archangel helps us to see love in situations where we feel that none exists. For example, if you are having difficult relationships with co-workers, bosses, or customers, ask Uriel to help you. He will guide you and the other people in miraculous ways so that you'll see the good that is inside all of us. With Uriel's help, you may forget why you were ever angry or fearful toward the people at work in the first place!

Folklore says that Uriel warned Noah of the impending flood. This archangel helps us during times of disaster, such as earthquakes, tornadoes, and torrential rains. Ask Uriel to help you whenever you feel fear about these situations. He may guide you to move to a different locale or prepare your home for maximum safety. Uriel also helps families to stay safe and intact during natural disasters.

Similarly, if your life feels like one giant shifting earthquake, ask for Uriel to re-orient your mind and thoughts to regain your peace of mind. Uriel is wonderful at rescuing us from our self-imposed crises, and he also helps us to establish a calm and centered life.

Uriel also helps us to fulfill our goals and dreams. He offers help completely, including giving us good ideas, keeping us encouraged and motivated, and helping us to manifest the material supplies we need for our project. Invite Uriel to become your partner in anything you are currently working on.

4. The Archangel Raphael, whose name means "God heals."

Raphael is in charge of all forms of healing. He supervises the healing needs of the earth and also its population. Raphael guides and helps people involved in the healing arts, such as doctors, practitioners, nurses, counselors, ecologists, and scientists. However, they can always ask for additional assistance, which Archangel Raphael is happy to provide!

If you currently work in a healing profession, you'll want to invite Raphael into your life. He will whisper guidance into your ear if you feel unsure about which direction to take with a patient. He also gives us creative ideas and needed information so that we can rapidly heal other people. Raphael intervenes during medical crises to ensure that miraculous "coincidences" line up all the right personnel and medical supplies with precious timing. This archangel is wonderful in helping scientists to create new breakthroughs in medical cures. So it's wise for all of us to pray for Raphael's help with health issues that confound the scientific community.

Those who aspire to become healers are the darlings of Archangel Raphael. This archangel knows that the earth needs many of these special people, and he miraculously helps would-be healers to enter their chosen profession. Raphael will help you to choose the best school for you, and he'll also guide you in creative ways to pay for your education. Leave all your concerns and worries about your future healing career to Raphael. He can more easily help you when you are free of tension and fear.

If you or a loved one needs healing, Raphael is the archangel to call upon. Except for cases where a person's death or illness is part of their overall divine plan, Archangel Raphael will deliver whatever they need to evoke a healing. So after you've called upon Raphael, you may receive sudden ideas, thoughts, or inspirations that give you just the right information to help in a healing. You'll want to pay attention to, and then follow, these angelically inspired answers to your prayers. Sometimes the angels don't swoop in and heal us. Instead, they may lead us to find humanly help for illnesses and accidents.

At other times, Raphael might point out to you that your thoughts have triggered the health problems. For example, Raphael may ask you to surrender old anger to him to release your body from the ravages of rage's poisonous effects. You'll then feel as comfortable in surrendering your anger as you would in disposing of yesterday's newspaper. When the anger is gone, your body becomes relieved of its anguish, and Raphael's legendary healing will have occurred again.

Raphael exudes a beautiful bright and clear emerald green light. This is the color of healing, and also of the heart chakra's love energy. As you call upon Raphael, you might see, with your inner eye, the emerald light surround you like a glorious rain shower of glowing light. Feel your cells drink in this quenching bath, and feel replenished and completely healed by its loving nourishment.

Raphael also has a second specialty: He guides and protects travelers of all sorts. Whether you are on a spiritual journey or about to embark to Europe, call upon Raphael to smooth the way.

To angels and archangels, no job is "big" or "small." All miracles are equally important to these beings who love us with all the might of God. All they ask, in return, is that we thank them for their help, share in their devotion to God, and that we fill our lives with joy and service.

♥ ♥ ♥

Nature Angels

The ancient spiritual text, *The Talmud*, says, "Every blade of grass has an angel bending over it saying, "Grow, grow." Imagine, then, how many angels are in your own backyard or a nearby park. Every blade of grass, flower, tree, sand grain, and raindrop has one or more angels overseeing its life-cycle. We also know nature angels as *faeries* and *devas*. These diminutive angels sing beautiful hymns as they tend to the needs of nature's growing bounty.

During my angel therapy sessions, the angels frequently advise my clients to spend more time in nature. One reason why angels prescribe "nature therapy" is its rapid healing effect. Imagine yourself sitting beneath the shade of tree with flowers and grass growing all around you. See yourself taking a deep breath and meditating upon God's glory, which is in and around you right now. Visualize the nature angels surrounding you with hugs and caresses, which heal every cell in your body and thought in your mind. Feel the gentle touch of the nature angels' loving embrace, as you imagine yourself in their midst.

If I feel stuck, drained, or fatigued, a brief sojourn to a natural setting restores my vitality and loving outlook. Try any natural setting that gives you some solitude, such as a lake or ocean shore, a mountain, a trail, or a forest area. Even an apartment balcony garden will do in a pinch. The nature angels live among the plants and mineral kingdom, no matter where.

Mentally alert the nature angels before you walk upon grass or ground, so they can move out of the way of your feet. Warn them, also, before you mow or spray your lawn. Nothing can harm a nature angel, in truth, since they have no physical bodies. They also have no fear or animosity, as they are pure love. However, you show the nature angels kindness and consideration by giving them ample time to scurry out of the path of your feet or lawnmower.

Animals, too, have angels around them. Your dog, cat, bird, or other pet has two or more guardian angels. You can commune with your pet's angels whenever you hug, pet, or play with your animal. Feel the special loving energy of these magnificent angels.

You'll probably agree that your own pet functions as an angel in your family. Many animals are on angelic assignment from God to provide solace, comfort, and companionship to us humans. Pets also perform the heavenly function of absorbing stress from our household, much like an air filter suctioning smoke out of a room. Angels, such as your pet, thrive on feeling loved and appreciated. They ask for so little, and yet give us so much in return.

❤ ❤ ❤

Asking for Angels

Sometimes, I'll see people whom an entourage of angels surrounds. I always stop them and ask whether they purposely called the angels. Always, the answer I hear is, "Yes, I asked to be surrounded by angels." The more we call upon the angels, the more they can come to our assistance.

Angels *want* to surround us, and they greatly desire to give us help. Our joy brings *them* enormous pleasure. Yet, they cannot help us unless we ask. A universal law that binds angels says, "No angel shall interfere with a human's life unless asked, with the sole exception of a life-threatening emergency. An angel will not make decisions for a human, but—when asked—an angel may offer advice and different ways of looking at the given situation." So an angel may nudge you or encourage you, and an angel may create a miraculous coincidence for you. However, an angel cannot help you unless you choose to accept the help, because you have free will.

To ask for angelic assistance, you needn't conduct a formal invocation ceremony. God and the angels aren't complicated, due to their true nature of pure and simple love. Only our lower-self ego believes that spirituality is necessarily complicated, because it cannot believe that something so powerful and great could be accessible to everyone instantly. Yet, it's true.

The angels hear the prayers of your heart, and just by your mental cry for help, they flock to your side. You can also consciously ask for more angels to surround you or your loved one. Parents can ask for angelic baby-sitters to guide and protect their children throughout the day. If a loved one is traveling, ask Raphael and the angels to watch over the journey.

Ask the angels to help your friends who are in need of comfort and direction.

Some ways to call upon the angels include:

- *Writing a letter to the angels.* Pour out your heart when discussing your confusions, hurts, and anxieties. Hold nothing back, so that the angels can help every part of you and your situation.

- *Visualizing.* Call it your inner eye, your imagination, or your third eye—the term doesn't matter. Visualizing angels is a powerful way to call them to your side. See the angels flying in circles around you or your loved ones. See powerful angels thronged by your side. See the room you are in crowded with thousands of angels. These visualizations are angelic invocations that create your reality.

  Angels are glowing with the light of love, so they don't have a physical form. However, angels can take on a physical appearance by projecting a mental image to us, if this will help us. So if you visualize cherubs, large glowing beings, or a beautifully dressed angelic woman, the angels will take on this form to help you recognize them.

- *Mentally calling upon angels.* Think, *Angels, please help me,* and they are with you instantly. If you are sincere in your call, the angels hear your mental cry for assistance. You can word your request as an affirmation, such as "I have hundreds of angels surrounding me now," or as a petitional prayer: "Angels, I am in pain and need your help now." You can ask God to send you angels, or you can call the angels directly.

- *Speaking to angels aloud.* You can verbalize your request, and sometimes we do this unconsciously, such as when we say, "Oh, God" during distress. You might find that spending time alone in a quiet setting, especially outdoors in nature, is a wonderful opportunity to have a verbal conversation with the angels.

♥ ♥ ♥

You Know That Angels Are Near When . . .

You *feel* the angels' presence. Perhaps you sense a warm brush across your face, shoulders, hands, or arms. You might feel their hug, or the brush of a wing across your skin. The air pressure changes when angels enter a room. There is a palpable thickening, as if a delicious cloud just rolled in to shield you from the heat. Also, the room temperature may seem to shift, or you might catch a whiff of a beautiful lilting fragrance that you can't quite identify. When the angels hug you, you feel a deep warmth flow through your chest, and your heart expands with unearthly love.

You *see* the angels' presence. The calling cards of angels are visible. A sparkle of white, blue, or green light out of the corner of your eye signals that an angel is near. A glowing shadow moving so fast that you wonder if it's your imagination is another signal. And the beautiful angels you see in a darkened room, or standing beside a beloved friend or teacher, confirm that the angelic kingdom visits you.

You *hear* the angels' presence—a loving whisper in your ear that urges you to improve your life. Or an unmistakable shout warning you to, "Watch out!" A voice inside your mind counseling you to reach for the stars, and the sweet strains of music coming from out of nowhere. These are the sounds that angels make.

You *know* the angels' presence. When you suddenly get an idea that dramatically transforms your life, an angel has just delivered a message from God and has tucked it safely within your heart. When you have an unmistakable knowingness that angels are near you, trust that it is so.

You *experience* the angels' presence. When they miraculously avert a near-tragedy, or a door "coincidentally" opens for you at just the right moment, you know that angels are helping you in the background. When you walk through nature and feel free and joy-filled, you can be sure that angels walk beside you along the way.

♥ ♥ ♥

Quieting the Mind

Our guardian angel continuously talks to us and gently offers advice and guidance. When we consciously ask for additional help and summon extra angels to our side, we receive an even steadier stream of divine communication. However, we must be aware of this heavenly assistance as it comes to us, *before* it can help us. Sometimes, chatter and noise so fill our thoughts that we can't hear the sweet and loving voice of our angels. The loud din of thoughts about our bills, family, and responsibilities overpowers the softer sound of the angels. We also ignore our angels' messages when they seem inappropriate to our current goals. For instance, if your angels urge you to relax and have fun, you may shrug off their advice with a "Haven't got the time" reply.

Many people also tell me they have difficulty meditating. Either they don't feel there's enough time for meditation, or their mind wanders or they fall asleep when they try to meditate.

While meditation certainly makes it easier to clearly hear your angels' messages, it's not an absolute necessity. There are other ways to quiet the mind sufficiently for the angelic voices to be heard.

For instance, you can slow your body, emotions, and thoughts by connecting with nature. If you can get in the habit of regularly looking out of the window of your home, office, or car and appreciating one bit of nature—a cloud, a tree, a bird chirping—you'll feel a wonderful quieting within yourself. Focus your eyes and mind on this miracle of nature before you, and feel your heart swell in appreciation and gratitude at its beauty. Better yet is when you actually spend time in nature. Of course, camping and hiking trips accomplish this nicely. But even a lunch break in a park or by the side of a brook is sufficient to re-establish your connection with Mother Earth, the nature angels, and your own guardian angels.

Another way to quiet the mind and body is by taking two or three slow and deep breaths. Breathe in as much as air as possible, then hold it in your lungs for a count of five or ten seconds. Then slowly breathe out. Repeat the breaths, and this time, picture yourself breathing in beautiful feelings such as relaxation, joy, and peace. When you breathe out, feel yourself releasing stress, tension, and worries.

You are *in*-spiring yourself with these deep breaths. In other words, you are filling yourself with the light of spirit. Dannion Brinkley, the author of *Saved by the Light,* who has had two near-death experiences, once told me that the spirit world communicates with us through our breaths. When we breathe in short, shallow spurts, we don't receive the depth of communication as we do when we really breathe deeply. Breathing is, in essence, our way of phoning home to heaven!

Eastern philosophies teach a visualization for quieting the mind in which you picture a large lake of clear water. Focus your attention in the center of the lake, as if you were underwater and easily breathing and floating as you looked at the water around you. Notice that sand granules are slowly floating to the bottom of the lake. As the sand falls, the water becomes perfectly clear and still. Feel your body and mind responding to this stillness, with all your cares and concerns gently falling and settling into a gentle quietness.

Physical exercise also has a quieting effect. Studies show that after we vigorously work out, our brain chemistry shifts in healthful directions. The post-exercise brain has increased amounts of the mood- and energy-altering neurotransmitter called "serotonin." Many people also report an increase in creative ideas and brainstorms while they are exercising. Probably, the increased breathing during exercise leads to this sort of *in*-spiration. Try 30 minutes of vigorous walking, bicycling, or an outdoor sport, and you'll find that angel communication comes quite naturally both during and after your workout.

It's easier to hear your angels when you are alone, especially when you are in a natural setting. We all need time-outs from the world to regenerate our energy and collect our thoughts. Make a daily appointment to spend time alone, when your mind isn't focused on some worldly task. Whether you sit in a meditative lotus position or engage in a creative activity such as painting, singing, dancing, or gardening, make time for yourself and your angels to commune together.

♥ ♥ ♥

How to Hear Your Angels' Messages

Not everyone "hears" angelic voices as audible sounds. Many people receive divine messages through nonverbal means such as visions, feelings, or a knowingness.

Hearing the voice of God and the angels is called *clairaudience,* which means "clear hearing." The voice may sound like your own or it may sound different. The voice can emanate from within your body, within your mind, or sound as if it's outside your head. When the angel warned me about my car being stolen, his voice sounded as if he were talking through a paper towel tube, just outside my right ear. While channeling the messages of this book, I heard the words both inside and outside my mind.

You might hear a faint voice and wonder what it said. In such cases, go ahead and ask your angels to repeat their message. Say to them, "A little louder, please." The angels appreciate your feedback, as they want to deliver clear and understandable guidance.

At first, you may believe that the voice is your imagination or wishful thinking. This is especially true when you begin consciously interacting with angels. You think, *This is a fantasy. I* wish *it were true that angels would help me, but I'm probably doing something wrong and the angels won't notice me.*

We heal this type of thinking through faith, trust, and practice. If your faith in angels is uncertain, ask God to help you. Pray, "Please help me to have more faith. I am willing to release all of my fears that keep me from having full faith." The Divine universe always fulfills requests for more faith.

Angelic voices are consistently loving and supportive, even when they warn us of impending danger or wrong turns. As a psychotherapist, I was trained to believe that hearing voices was a sign of insanity. Yet, the voice of the ego is the only source of "insanity." Ego voice messages are always destructive, abusive, and impulsive. For example, the ego may try to convince you that you'll fail. The ego also changes its mind constantly, so it will tell you to do one thing Monday, another thing Tuesday, and a completely different thing Wednesday. If you listen to the voice of the ego, your life will be chaotic and fear-filled.

Angelic voices, in contrast, patiently repeat the guidance to us day after day until we finally follow it. You may hear your angels tell you for years that you would be a great healer or author, for example. Or your angels may repeatedly ask you to take better care of your body. You know that the guidance comes from angels when it is loving, focused, not hurtful to you or your family, and consistent.

Clairaudience is just one of the four ways we receive angelic assistance, however. Your angels may speak to you in pictures and visual mental images. We call this *clairvoyance,* or "clear seeing." Angelic messages may come to you as single snapshot images, either in your mind or outside your mind. Or, you may see miniature scenes, as if from a movie. The images may be black-and-white or full color. Angelic visual messages can be symbolic, such as seeing a stop sign as a signal that you should take a rest, slow, or stop what you are doing.

Intuitively, you might readily understand what the visual images mean. For instance, you might see an image of a trophy, and instinctively you know this means that success is ahead for you. If you have trouble understanding your angelic visual guidance, be sure to ask for assistance. Ask your angels to clarify their message, and continue asking for clarification until you are completely certain of their meaning.

Sometimes we shut down our angelic channels of communication due to fear. You might see an image of your future that frightens you, and you turn off your clairvoyance by shutting the third eye's eyelid. Many years ago, I was an uneducated housewife who was unhappy because I wanted to make a contribution to the world but didn't feel qualified to do anything meaningful.

Then God and the angels gave me mental visual images of the life I was meant to lead. I saw myself writing self-help books and appearing on talk shows. The images showed me having an advanced college degree. These visions scared me a great deal because I didn't feel capable of fulfilling them. I thought that I lacked the intelligence, time, and money to create the meaningful life shown in the clairvoyant images.

I found that I could shut off the visions by eating a lot of food. My full stomach interrupted my telephone connection with God and the angels. However, when my stomach digested the food, I'd feel irritable because I would see the contrast between my present life and the life I was supposed to live. Fortunately, I got tired of dodging my divine guidance, and surrendered to God. When I did, He began opening doors before me, one step at a time. The angels arranged for me to achieve every part of the visions I saw, in ways I could have never planned or anticipated.

One of my clients shut down her clairvoyance when, as a young girl, she saw a visual image of her parents divorcing in the future. Another client closed her third eye because she foresaw herself having an affair with a married co-worker, and she wanted to continue her interactions with him while wearing blinders to the truth. One of my other clients was trying to ignore a steady angelic voice within that counseled, "It's time to look for work at a different place," because she didn't trust God to fulfill her material needs during the job transition.

You might also shut off your clairvoyance if you are afraid of what you *might* see. As much as you want to see your angels in person, you might harbor a deep-seated fear that seeing a "ghost" would be terrifying. Your angels honor such fears, and you won't see angelic apparitions until you feel confident that such a vision would comfort—not frighten—you.

The third way we receive angelic guidance is through our emotions and physical sensations. We call this *clairsentience,* or "clear feeling." Clairsentients get divine guidance through bodily sensations, such as a tightening of the jaw, fists, stomach, or sex organs. They intuitively know the specific meaning of these tightening reactions. A clairsentient feels air pressure and room temperature changes that warn him or her of negative situations.

Each of our five senses has a corresponding spiritual sense. Clairsentients receive angelic guidance through an etheric sense of smell, taste, and touch. You may know that your beloved deceased grandmother is near when you smell her perfume or favorite flower. An angel may shower your room with the aroma of orange blossoms to tell you of an impending wedding.

Clairsentients receive a lot of guidance through their intuition, gut feelings, and hunches. Much of our intuition comes from the stomach region, and the stomach flutters, relaxes, and tightens according to the angelic guidance. Instinctively, the clairsentient interprets the meaning of these gut feelings, and a *wise* clairsentient follows these internal directives without hesitation.

Clairsentients get angelic messages through their heart and love emotions, as well. If a thought of doing something swells your chest with warm feelings of joy, this is a directive from God and the angels. You may say, "Oh, this is too good to be true; I'm just dreaming," but the joy that your thought has brought you is a road map leading you to the life you are meant to have.

We call the fourth means of angelic communication *claircognizance,* or "clear knowing." Men are frequently claircognizant, and they may not even realize that they naturally receive detailed and accurate information from God and the angels. You can ask a claircognizant a question on almost any topic in the world. Within minutes, he will give you an accurate answer, completely supported by facts and figures. You might ask, "How did you know that?" and he'll answer, "I don't know! A few minutes ago, I didn't know that information."

Claircognizants know, without knowing *how* they know. Consequently, they may doubt the validity of their knowingness. This is a mistake, because when divine wisdom enters our mind, it is a gift we can use to improve our life and to serve the world.

We all have access to all four channels of communication. Usually, we have one primary means of receiving angelic guidance and one secondary—or lesser—channel of communication. With practice, you can become adept at receiving messages in all four ways. In the beginning stages of speaking to your angels, though, most people concentrate upon their natural means of communication.

Naturally visually oriented people will want to pay attention to their mental visions. If you tend to focus upon sounds, then listen for inner or outer words, voices, and auditory messages. If you tend to be a touchy-feely type, your emotions and bodily sensations are the instruments that relay divine guidance to you. And if you are intellectually inclined, or a person who constantly searches for hidden meanings in situations, then you'll want to monitor your thoughts for those heavenly moments of "knowingness" that bring you certainty in guiding your actions.

♥ ♥ ♥

Some Ways to Communicate with Angels

From the angels:

"We aren't that difficult to hear, if you will listen for us with an open heart. Most of the time, we are closer to you than you can imagine. A whisper, a thought, is the only signal we need from you to get a conversation started. We have enormous respect for what you're going through here on planet Earth at this time. We never seek to interfere with your lives, only to bring you blessings of insights and new ways of looking at yourselves."

You can communicate with angels in a variety of ways, including automatic writing, dreamwork, oracle cards, and intuitional or psychic communication. It's important to choose a communication style to which you feel naturally drawn. Anything that feels forced or frightening will block your ability to clearly hear your angels' messages. Also, angel communication takes a little practice and patience at first. So, you'll want to try methods that you are likely to stick with for a while.

While reading the following descriptions, pay attention to your reactions to each method. Ask yourself, "Do I feel happy or excited about trying it? Or, do I feel neutral or even negative about this method?" Then try the methods that appeal to you.

— *Automatic writing*. I received the angels' messages in this book through this process. It means that the angels literally write their message through the channeler. Automatic writing can involve a form of dictation, in which you hear the angelic voices and then write what you hear. The voice may be inside or outside your head. It may or may not sound like your own voice. You'll likely be conscious of what you are writing in this form of automatic writing.

Another type of automatic writing involves the angels physically pushing your hand while you use a pencil or type on a keyboard. Most people who automatically write this way are unaware of the words they are writing. This is the form of automatic writing used in this book.

You can try this second form of automatic writing by taking these steps:

1. Set a definite time and date when you will attempt to channel with automatic writing. Mentally tell your angels of this appointment so they can prepare. Then, be sure to follow your promised schedule.

2. Choose a quiet place where you won't be interrupted. Turn off the phone and put a sign on the door so others won't make noises that will block your communication flow. It's best to have quiet background music or a tape of nature sounds, and also some pleasant fragrance such as fresh flowers or incense in the room.

3. If you plan to try automatic writing with a pencil, you'll need a seating arrangement that allows you to comfortably hold the pencil over a paper on a steady surface. As you begin automatic writing, you want to make it easy on yourself. So, you probably won't want to try

automatically writing upon a pad of paper on the floor, on your lap, or another position where the pencil doesn't easily flow.

Some automatic writers use pens; however, pencils are traditional since they don't skip or bleed. Several years ago, "planchettes" were used to hold pencils for automatic writers. Planchettes are wooden triangles with a hole in the center, supported by three ball bearings that allow smooth movement in any direction. The pencil is placed firmly in the planchette's hole, and the spirit world guides the channeler's hand to push the planchette, much like on a Ouija board.

You might opt to conduct automatic writing with a computer or typewriter keyboard instead of with pencil and paper. No special seating arrangements are necessary for this beyond your normal chair, desk, and keyboard.

4. Make sure that you are comfortable. It's best to wear nonbinding clothing, and it's important to channel on a slightly empty stomach without the influence of *any* stimulants (coffee, colas, sugar, herbs, chocolate) or depressants (heavy meals, alcohol, drugs, herbs).

5. Take two or three very deep breaths. Say a prayer such as *The Lord's Prayer,* or an affirmation such as, "I see myself surrounded by white light and divine love. I am safe, protected and loved." You may want to ask Archangel Michael to oversee your channeling, especially at first when you may not be able to readily discern an earthbound spirit from an angel. Michael will act as a doorman who only allows invited guests to enter your territory.

6. At this point, you may immediately feel the channeling sensation begin. Don't let it frighten you. The first time I tried automatic writing with a pencil, it began rapidly moving on its own, which startled me. My fear then blocked the whole channeling process for a long time. In the beginning, the pencil will write circular doodles. These circles are the angels' way of expressing their great joy at making a connection with you. After you and the angels become accustomed to working together, then letters, words, and sentences will come through your pencil. Usually, though, the pencil will write circles for the first one to three days that you try automatic writing.

Or, you may hear an inner voice and feel a tug that pushes you to write what you hear. The automatic writing can also take a more tactile approach. If you are writing at a keyboard, the sensation may feel like a piano teacher grasping your hands and pushing your fingers onto the appropriate keys. Or, you could receive intuitive impulses that give you an emotional feeling about what you should write. Your angelic messages may also come as visions, and you may feel guided to write about what you see. If you are a claircognizant, you will receive chunks of information from the angels. You will have certainty of the facts of your knowledge, without knowing "how" you know.

Trance and semi-trance channelers aren't aware of the writing that occurs through them. A full-trance channel actually loses awareness of her surroundings. She feels a sensation of being lifted away from her body while the spirit world channels through her. My channeling is in a semi-trance state, where I am aware of my "me-ness," but unaware of most of the messages coming through me. I also lose track of time and place during most of my channelings. I will think that 20 minutes has gone by, when actually several hours have passed.

The main point with automatic writing is to flow with whatever sensations you receive. Your impressions may come as visions, words, information, or emotional or physical feelings. Or you may receive a combination of these various communications. Practice really does make perfect with automatic writing, so do not allow yourself to become discouraged just because your first few messages don't seem coherent. If you initially get superficial messages, that's okay, too. At first, you'll want to concentrate on becoming comfortable with the process of automatic writing. Then, you'll naturally move on to gathering meaningful communications from the spirit world.

When you become tired, disoriented, or feel any pain, it's important to stop your channeling. Many people limit their channeling time to an hour or less at first. Allow yourself time to build up to longer automatic writing periods.

If you ever find yourself channeling a spirit that belittles you, or pushes you to do anything that would cause pain to you or another, stop. You are not channeling angels at that point. Angels would never give messages that cause emotional, physical, or psychic pain. Call in Archangel Michael and ask him to clear away the earthbound spirit which you are channeling. Do not fight the spirit with fear or anger, but do say prayers and visualize yourself surrounded with white light before having another channeling session. Your greatest ally in the channeling arena is your determination to channel only love. Nothing that is from love can ever hurt you.

— ***Dreamwork***. As the angels clearly spelled out in their chapter entitled, "Sleep," we interact a lot with the angelic kingdom during our dreams. You'll increase your number of angel messages and the speed of your clearing work simply by inviting the angels into your dreams.

For example, if you are undecided about your career direction, mentally say a prayer similar to this as you lay your head on your pillow:

"Angels, please enter my dreams tonight and give me clear messages, which I will remember, to help me to know which direction to take with my career."

They always meet this request, and you will likely have a lucid dream that you easily remember, in the hour right before you awaken. Or, the angels may help you in your sleep in such a way that you don't recall your dream's contents. Yet, you awaken and know that something shifted within you during the night. You feel happier, more positive, and much clearer about which direction to take. This is a sign that the angels have re-arranged your thoughts and beliefs, to help you release fears that keep you indecisive about your career.

If you feel blocked in any area of your life, write this message on a piece of paper and place it under your pillow. Repeat the phrase mentally three times as you are falling asleep:

"Dearest Angels,
I ask you to work with me in my sleep tonight, to clear away any blocks that keep me from fully enjoying my life. Please either call these blocks to my

*attention, or completely remove them from my
mind, emotions, and body during tonight's sleep.*
Thank you."

In the morning, you'll awaken refreshed, but with an
awareness that you've worked during the night. You
may not recall the details of your angelic nocturnal
work, but you will feel it deeply. Your head may even
feel funny, because of the restructuring that occurred
overnight. Still, any blocks that the angels carted
away were heavy weights impeding you from your
life's plan and purpose. You'll feel grateful that you
asked for this clearing, and you may want to invite the
angels into your dreams nightly.

— *Divination Tools.* Oracle cards and pendulums provide
a tangible means for communicating with the angels. If
you are clairsentient—that is, one who receives intu-
itions through physical and emotional feelings—these
methods will feel quite natural to you.

• *Oracle cards.* You can purchase angel-themed
oracle cards at most bookstores. There are different
brand names of angel cards, and you'll likely feel
drawn to one or two particular sets. This internal
pull will help you decide which set to buy, as it
shows which cards you share a natural affinity and
resonance with. Many metaphysical bookstores
have sample card decks that you can examine before making your final purchase decisions. Some
angel oracle cards are based upon the ancient tarot
deck. Angel cards feature colorful paintings of
archangels, cherubs, and seraphim, along with

words or sentences describing the meaning of each particular card.

To communicate with angels using oracle cards, meditate while shuffling the deck, and mentally ask the angels to give you assistance. I like to light incense and play soft meditative background music as I use the angel oracle cards. As you shuffle the deck, you can ask your angels specific questions, request that they offer guidance about your life, or ask them to help you foresee your future. The angels tell you when to stop shuffling the deck. If you are clairsentient, you *feel* when it's time to stop shuffling. You also feel whether you should lay out certain cards or whether you should take the cards from the top of the deck. If you are clairaudient, you hear angels tell you to stop shuffling. Their voices may speak a number such as "seven," signaling that you are to lay out seven cards. Clairvoyants see visual cues, such as cards sticking out of the deck in a certain way as you shuffle them, as a signal to spread out the cards. This visual orientation also tells clairvoyants which cards to spread out. Claircognizants *know* when the time is right to spread out the cards, and which cards to lay out.

People who have a combination of communication channels use a variety of spiritual senses while shuffling the cards and spreading them out. For example, my clairsentience helps me to feel when to stop shuffling, then a clairaudient voice tells me how many cards to spread out. I clairvoyantly see the meaning of the card spreads. With prayer and practice, anyone can become skillfully adept at reading oracle cards—*especially* with the help of the angels.

You can spread the angel oracle cards according to the formations suggested in the card deck's instruction booklet. One classic card spread, for instance, involves laying out three cards. The first card shows your present life circumstances. The second card represents an obstacle or challenge you must surmount, and the third card reveals your best possible outcome after you overcome your challenge.

I use several different angel oracle card sets simultaneously. I spread out one row of cards from the first set horizontally. Then, I spread another row horizontally below the second set, and so on. After I've spread five sets of cards, I read the cards vertically. I look at the first card in the upper left-hand corner and know that this is the primary issue concerning my client. Then I look at the cards vertically below the first card and look for a "theme" among the cards in each row. Each vertical row's theme tells a story about my client's life purpose, emotional blocks, and future.

- *Pendulums.* This is a crystal or gem stone, such as jade, attached to a fine chain or satin rope. You hold the chain or rope and allow the stone to dangle until it hangs motionlessly. When you ask your angels questions, the stone will move in one certain direction as a "yes" response, and it will move in the opposite direction if the answer is "no." To discover which direction the stone travels to signal "yes" and "no," ask a question that you already know the answer to, such as "Is my name Susan?" or "Do I live in Ohio?" Watch which direction the stone moves, and you will establish its "yes" and "no" pattern. Once you establish the pendulum's "language," you can ask the angels to answer other questions. You'll find that a strong "yes" or "no" answer makes the stone move in very strong and wide swings. Some people, through practice and intuition, can determine more detailed answers than "yes" and "no" from the pendulum's movement.

— *Asking for Signs.* In your meditations, ask your angels to give you a clear sign in answer to your prayers. Usually, it's best not to outline which particular sign you want. Instead, your angels will signal you in an unmistakable way. You will notice and *know* that it's the sign you ask for.

The sign may come in nature, such as a feather falling from the sky, a bird soaring close to you, or a rainbow. Your sign can come from the ethers, such as a sudden fragrance, music, or flash of light that has no physical origin. Angel signs also include out-of-the-blue opportunities, like a phone call or letter delivering good news, or a book that jumps off the shelf as you walk by. Or your signs can come psychically, such as a vision, a dream, a voice, or an intuition.

Whatever sign you get, *trust in it.* Know that the angels always answer your prayers, requests, and calls. All we have to do is ask.

— *Verbal Channeling.* The angels will speak *through* you, if you like. When you verbally channel angels, their messages are spoken with your mouth and voice.

Sometimes, during my sessions, I channel my clients' angels instead of relaying their messages. My clients know that when the messages in our sessions contain phrases such as, "We believe that you would enjoy..." or "We counsel you to..." that the angels are talking, instead of just me.

If you are a healer, or involved in the creative arts, you've probably already channeled angels. Perhaps you were talking, healing, or creating, and suddenly a wonderful, novel idea comes out of you. Afterward, you wonder, "Where did that come from?" The answer is, of course, from the angels.

To verbally channel the angels, use the relaxation and protective prayer techniques outlined in the section about "automatic writing." Mentally hold a clear intention of wanting the angels to speak through your vocal cords and mouth. Stay in a relaxed and positive frame of mind, as skepticism blocks the angels from communicating through you.

As you feel an impulse to speak, do not allow your mind to wander into fears or doubts. Simply begin speaking, with a sense of trust or adventure. It's a little like the first time you ride a bicycle. The angels will use your vocabulary as they speak through you, as if they are pushing keys on a typewriter to form coherent messages. Some verbal channelers are aware of the messages being spoken through them; others are not. Either way, you'll want to tape-record your channelings, or speak to another person so you can review the verbal channelings later.

You'll know that you are channeling angels by their telltale signature of:

- *A very high, fine frequency.* Your head may feel some pressure, as if you are singing a very high note.

- *Loving, positive words, phrases, and messages.* Angels may warn you of danger or ask you to stop an unhealthful habit. But always, they word their advice in a "you can do it" coaching style.

- *Consistently reinforced, sequential messages.* Your angels will ask you to complete one step at a time as they counsel you to improve your life. They will patiently ask you to fulfill each step and may repeat the same message until you complete their request. After you've finished one step, the angels will applaud you and then give you another suggested step to take.

❤ ❤ ❤

Hearing Your Guardian Angel's Name

You'll interact with hundreds or even thousands of different angels throughout your lifetime. Some angel groups with which you work will remain consistent. At other times, you'll be accompanied by angels who are completely new to you.

Since angels are not after personal glory because they know that we are all united with God, they don't seek credit for their heavenly deeds. So most of the time, you won't be aware of the personal characteristics of the individual angels who are helping you. You can, however, get to know your guardian angel or angels, who are with you from physical birth to death.

Your guardian angels have names. Sometimes, they have human-sounding names. For example, my guardian angel is "Frederique." Other times, angels have descriptive names such as "Joy" or "Peace."

Ask your angels to tell you their names. Then be very still and listen. The answer may come intuitively, and you'll get a feeling about the name. Or you may hear a voice, see a vision, or simply "know" the name. If the message isn't clear enough for you to understand, ask your angels to repeat their names until you've got them. Never fear that your angels will be offended or run away if you say, "Could you repeat your answer a little louder, please?"

I met a woman who decided to ask for her angel's name as she was driving home from church one day. After she asked her angel, "What's your name?" the woman heard a little voice within her mind and heart reply, "Angel." The woman thought, "Angel! How can an angel be named 'Angel'?" So she asked her angel to repeat the answer a little louder and clearer, so she could be sure and really understand it. Again, the woman heard the same reply: "Angel."

The woman thought this was an odd name for an angel— a little like a cat being named "Cat." So she asked her angel to give her a sign if "Angel" truly was her name. At that instant, the woman felt compelled to look over her right shoulder as she was driving. There, in front of her was a huge sign that she had never before noticed. It read "Angel Motel." That's how she knew for sure that her guardian angel's name was "Angel."

♥ ♥ ♥

Trusting the Angels

"I *knew* that's what my angels were saying to me!"

My clients repeat this phrase to me practically every week, in one form or another. When I relay what I hear their angels saying, my clients often admit that they are aware of this advice. The angels may have urged my client to change jobs, take better care of her body, forgive her father, or move to a different locale. Very often, my clients admit the wisdom of the angelic advice, then add a "But . . ."

"But I don't have enough time or money."

"But I might fail and feel humiliated, and things might be worse than they are now."

"But what if the angels are wrong?"

"But what if God is really trying to trick me into a life of austere poverty and suffering?"

Just as the Law of Free Will prevents angels from helping us unless we ask, the same law means that we have the right to accept or reject the angelic assistance offered to us. Most of us would not consciously reject an angel's help. Still, we might mistakenly allow fear to talk us out of receiving good graciously.

After all, many of us grew up with teachings that implied that it's not right for us to accept gifts freely. We might have been scolded for not saying "Thank you" when someone gave us a present. Or perhaps we learned, "You can't get something for nothing," so we feel suspicious when someone—even an angel—offers to help us. We might wonder, "What's the catch?" as if God will ask us to reciprocate the favor in ways involving hardships or austerity.

Know that you *deserve* help from God and the angels! You are a precious and holy child of God, and we all deserve good.

If you have, or if you had, children, wouldn't you want the very best for them? Also, let's keep in mind that our higher selves are eternally one with God. So, in essence, when God gives to us, He is giving to His own self.

Never think that the angels are too busy to help you. Don't believe for a moment that your needs are too petty or trivial for the kingdom of heaven to intervene. This is just our lower-self ego, pushing away help, because of deep-seated feelings of unworthiness. Your true self knows that you are very, very worthy. Your true self knows that we are all part of the divine perfection that is God.

If asking for, and accepting, divine assistance feels unnatural to you, ask your angels to help you change this tendency. Angels can heal away low self-esteem and any personality characteristic that gives you hardships. They will gladly roll away the stones that block you from fully enjoying your divine inheritance, which is your birthright from your holy Creator.

♥ ♥ ♥

Heavenly Surroundings

Your angels are with you wherever you go, so they aren't concerned about *where* you choose to talk to them. It's just that certain types of environments make it so much easier to hear their voices.

When I first started talking to my angels, they urged me to buy some classical music tapes and some fresh flowers for my office. I balked at spending good money on flowers that would soon wilt, or for music that is freely available on the radio. Still, the angels urged me to stop at a florist shop and buy flowers, and to then go to a music store and buy a tape. They were quite specific!

Finally, I asked them what this was all about. They explained that, although my angel statues and pictures in my office set the atmosphere for an angelic conference, it would be better if I decorated with items from the *invisible* realm. Music, fragrance, and color are composed of vibrations that shift our minds into a higher level, where we can more readily understand our angels' messages. Radio music is fine, but all the commercial interruptions interfere with the angels' music coming through.

So I purchased some tapes by Beethoven, Handel, and Vivaldi. Many baroque composers have strong connections with spirituality. For example, Antonio Vivaldi was a priest who spent his lifetime teaching orphans how to play music. George Handel told the king of England that angels helped him compose his famous "Hallelujah Chorus." The music felt as if angels channeled it. I instantly understood why they were so anxious for me to surround myself with glorious chamber music.

Months later, I discovered scientific research that supported what my angels already knew: People have more statistically verified accounts of telepathy when soft music plays in their room. I've also noticed that, when I play audiocassettes of nature sounds, my mind lifts as if I were actually outside.

I also took the angels' advice and bought the most fragrant flowers I could find, which turned out to be tuberoses and star gazers. These beautiful perfumey flowers lifted my spirits. I loved their fragrance so much that I'd bring my vase of flowers from my home office to my nightstand so I could smell them all night. Always, the flowers inspire wondrous dreams and easier interactions with the angels.

Today, I also burn incense when I'm consciously contacting the angels. Beautiful, flowery incense also elevates the spirit and increases the vibrations so that channeling is easier.

Lighting is also part of the invisible realm, since the rays and beams emitted by candles and colored bulbs are not tangible. The angels suggest using an assortment of lighting in your meditation area. Angels resonate with any lighting that is soft and natural, but they also appreciate playfully colored lights because they cast a fun mood. And you've read how much the angels enjoy us relaxing and having fun!

♥ ♥ ♥

Developing the Habit of Asking
Your Angels for Help

From the angels:

"We speak to you continuously, nonstop from on high. We gleefully join you in fun times, and cheer you in the sad ones. We beseech you to listen further, for we can boost you in ways yet unknown. We help you in countless and numerous occasions, and our 'thanks' is your happiness. When you truly delight in opening your ears to The Angelic Realm, you will experience a music in your life beyond all comparison. If you could know how delightful your life can truly be, you would wait no longer to hear our beck and call!"

The angels *want* to communicate clearly with you. They have so much to give you! They can bring you information, guidance, protection, moral support, and a pat on the back. In fact, they continuously try to do just that. Yet, a giver cannot give unless there is a willing recipient. Are you willing to receive the glorious good that is being given you right now?

One way to become more receptive to angelic communication and assistance is by clearing any blocks you may have that prevent you from receiving. Write, read, and say the following affirmations several times a day, and within two weeks, you will heal much of your resistance to angelic help:

"I graciously accept good into my life."
"I am willing to release all fears of receiving love."
"It is safe for me to be loved and cared for."
"I deserve love and assistance."

If you're accustomed to taking care of everyone else, you'll need to be patient with yourself while you develop the new habit of accepting help from the angels. Sometimes it doesn't feel safe to receive assistance. Perhaps you fear that if you don't do everything yourself, others won't need you. You may also fear losing control of the situation if you aren't taking charge of everything yourself. You might worry that the angels are too busy to help you or that you don't "deserve" angelic assistance. Or, you just may automatically do things on your own and need reminders to ask your angels for help.

All these blocks to angelic intervention are understandable and very, very normal. If you simply forget to ask your angels for help, place visual reminders around your home, car, and office. Angel statues, cards, and posters give cues to jog your memory whenever you need help.

If you are aware that, deep down, you have blocks that prevent you from asking for help, the angels can heal these blocks away:

If you need more faith or belief, ask God and the angels to help you!

If you feel undeserving of Divine intervention, ask God and the angels to help you!

If you worry that your problems are too "trivial" for heavenly help, ask God and your angels anyway. Remember that God and The Angelic Realm can help everybody simultaneously, since time and space do not limit them. Your request for Divine help doesn't pull God or the angels away from helping somebody else.

Whatever you need, God and the angels can help!

Remember: God and the angels love you, and they love to help you so that you can easily feel, enjoy, and give love.

❤ ❤ ❤

Purifying the Channels of
Divine Communication

From the angels:

"You can hear us so much more clearly when you purify the air around you. Think of divine communication as coming through a mist, which is really the buffer in the atmosphere differentiating one spiritual realm from another. The finer the mist, the easier the communication between us can be. But a dense mist covering prevents us from clearly hearing your thoughts and seeing your deeds, and is more likely to create misunderstandings about our intentions for you. By purifying yourself, to the extent you are able, we are joyful because we are much more reachable as far as you are concerned, when the mist around you is refined and purified."

When the angels talk about "purifying the air around you," they aren't referring to clean air in the traditional sense. They mean, instead, that your thoughts and lifestyle actions affect your aura and the energy field around you. It's a little like clearing the static from a telephone line so you can hear callers more clearly. Angelic communication is easier to understand when you purify your aura and energy field.

All purification steps are best if they come from your desire and willingness. It's best not to force yourself to take any step that feels like you are "denying yourself." Only undergo those steps for which you feel ready. Undertake these new habits with the joy of knowing that they bring you to a closer understanding of your true God-self nature.

— Purify your thoughts.

From the angels:

"We're not asking you to try to be a saint upon the earth, but do your best to monitor the words, phrases, and ideas you speak to yourself and to others. Any fear-based thought, such as jealousy, competition, resentment, victimhood, or retaliation, makes your energy field dense and dark. Unforgiveness—toward yourself, a situation, a person, or a public figure or agency— blackens your aura like thick smoke."

I have clairvoyantly seen what thought-forms look like. Immediately after you have a thought, you release a bubblelike object with a life of its own. The size of the thought-form seems to correspond to how much energy you put behind the thought. Thought-forms serve your every command. They go out into the world and create whatever you've thought about.

For instance, a client of mine really wanted a certain job. During the job interview, I saw her release a huge thought-form that looked like a thick, shimmering soap bubble about four feet tall by one foot wide. It had a life force of its own, and a forward thrust energy. When my client called me a week later to report that she'd successfully secured her new job, I wasn't surprised. The energy she'd released into the world marked "This is the job I desire," guaranteed that she'd receive her wish.

There are no neutral thoughts, nor are there moments in the day when your thoughts don't create thought-forms and their causative effects. Your fearful thoughts act like bloodthirsty henchmen that bring terror back to you, their master. Your loving thoughts obediently bring you joyful situations and relations. It's your choice.

Many people who are drawn to channel angels feel the need to avoid negative media. So, they may stop watching television, listening to the radio, or reading the newspaper. They may become distanced from friends who chronically complain, and they may choose to leave careers that feel inconsistent with a positive outlook.

Channeling angels requires that our thoughts be attuned to the highest frequency of love. Any worries or fears interfere with our channeling abilities, as these thought-forms create static on our psychic telephone line. In the chapter called "Angel Therapy," you can read about a very effective method for quickly releasing these ego-self thoughts.

— *Purify your motives.* Give your motivations to God and the angels and ask that they be purified. You can do this simply by asking God to help you. Say, "God, I give you my motivations and ask your help in purifying them so all my motives are aligned with truth and love." Very soon, you will feel a strong sense of relief, as the Love reorganizes your thoughts and feelings. A deep sense of peace and order follows this.

Your highest motivation is to give glory to God in all ways. Of course, since your higher self is one with God, you are actually giving glory to the *true you*, along with the true self of every other child of God. Lower-self motivations occur when you believe that you want to give glory to yourself alone, as a special person. Everyone is equally special. So, when we want a *separate* specialness, we trigger the pain and loneliness that comes from believing we are separated from God and our spiritual siblings.

— *Purify your actions.* Before doing anything, ask your higher self, God, and the angels to guide you. Know that this Divine guidance will direct your actions from the one power of love. In this way, you are assured of continually floating in a sea of miracles that will astound you in their beauty. You will always be in the right place at the right time.

— *Purify your home.* Environments absorb negative energy, which comes from a variety of fear-based sources. Anything tinged with fear that is in your home—newspapers, magazines, mail, television programs, radio talk shows, arguments among family members, or fearful thoughts held by past occupants of the house—can bring dark energy into your surroundings.

You'll want to clear your home, office, or any environment you frequent. Clearing allows the light to freely circulate and lifts your surroundings' energy to the highest level possible. Some ways to purify your home include painting the walls; shampooing the carpet or recarpeting; placing bowls of rubbing alcohol in every room of the house for a minimum of 24 hours; setting clear quartz crystals in the sunlight for four hours (to clear them of negative energy) and then putting the crystals in different rooms of your home; and burning sage weed or incense throughout each room.

Still, perhaps the best way to clear any environment is by calling upon the angels. Mentally ask for Archangel Michael and his Band of Mercy to circulate the area and draw away all dark energy or earthbound spirits. You may be able to see Michael with your spiritual vision. If so, you'll watch him lead other angels in a posse, gathering all lower-energy forms that could interfere with your divine communication and joyful living.

— *Purify your relationships.* Although you've undoubtedly experienced pain in relationships, you have the choice of healing the residual emotions to clear any heaviness or darkness. This is an important part of the clearing work that will help you to easily have conversations with your angels. Whether you carry old pain from your childhood, adolescence, or recent past, you can release negativity that holds you back.

The angels first remind you that every negative feeling you hold toward another has a boomerang effect. It is impossible to judge or blame another person and not feel emotional pain. As much as we would like to see ourselves as separate from a person we view as "bad," ultimately such a separation is impossible. We are united with each other—forever. That is why you feel depressed when you become angered at another person. The anger you send outward acts like a laser beam pointed toward a mirror, and it instantly comes back and hits you.

Other people are our mirrors! When the angels speak of the necessity of forgiving, they don't want you to forgive because of moral codes. They know that judgment, blame, and anger are burdens upon your soul. They ask you to unburden yourself, and this is the true definition of forgiveness. It means setting yourself free.

If you don't feel ready to forgive someone's actions,

then forgive the person instead. See that person through the eyes of an angel. The guardian angel sees only the good, the truth, the Godness of that other person. Angels look past the surface personality, errors, and mistakes of a person and see straight into the individual's heart. If you've read about or experienced a near-death experience, you've heard about the guide that accompanies us. This guardian angel's unconditional and all-consuming love burns away all fear from those who are crossing over to heaven.

You, too, can have a great healing effect upon the world—and simultaneously heal your relationship with yourself and all others—by modeling yourself after the guardian angels' viewpoint. The more you train your mind to see the angel residing within each person, the more you will know and appreciate the angel who *you* are in truth.

— *Purify your schedule.* We sometimes procrastinate spiritual growth by creating a busy schedule. Busyness ensures that there is no time to explore the inner self. For that reason, the angels ask us to purify our schedules by eliminating unnecessary or redundant activities.

You may want to take an inventory for two days and write down how you spend your time. Then look for areas of wasted time. We don't mean relaxation, since the angels definitely believe resting is a worthwhile activity. Instead, look for the moments where you are busy, with no meaningful results. These are the activities you engage in out of habit or fear. Once you identify your habitual time-wasters, you'll probably easily change to healthier habits.

However, if you are staying busy out of fear, you may

resist the angelic guidance to restructure the way you spend your time. After all, when you are continuously active, there's no time to think about your life purpose, your true self, and God. Yet, these are such important endeavors, aren't they? After all, nothing is more important than fulfilling the sacred mission for which you were born! Nothing in this world yields even a fraction of the joy compared to your life of right livelihood and right relations.

If you write your top five priorities—in other words, what is truly important to you—you can compare these areas to your actual schedule. Then ask yourself, "Am I spending my time in ways that fulfill my priorities?" If not, then diligently seek ways to cut out time-wasters, and replace the new gaps in your schedule with something more personally meaningful to you. You'll find that purifying your schedule heightens your energy and enthusiasm level more than just about any other step you can take.

The angels strongly counsel you to spend time alone in nature as frequently as possible. Make this one of your top priorities. The healing effect of nature, combined with time alone, gives the perfect opportunity for you to really hear your true self, God, and the angels speak to you. The nature angels will soothe and comfort you. In this natural setting, you'll more easily hold honest conversations with yourself and the divine spiritual realm.

— *Purify your body.* If you are being called to channel angels, you have undoubtedly received inner guidance about your diet and lifestyle. This guidance urges you to eliminate sugar, stimulants, meats, alcohol, dairy products, or other foods from your diet. These are very real messages, sent to you from heaven.

Their dietary advice is part of answers to prayers in which you asked for help in hearing the voices of God and the angels. The reason why your angels intervene into your diet is that your body is being prepared for a reattunement. The vibrational frequency of angels is at such a high and fine level, that your body must be retuned before you can hear them. It's similar to tuning a piano, so that when the pianist's finger strikes its keys, the piano can emit harmonious music.

God is calling you to be a transmitter of angelic messages. Your nervous system can only handle the angels' frequency if your body vibrates at a sufficiently high level. A poor diet creates static on the angelic communication lines, so your angels ask you to purify your body. You may receive the angels' dietary suggestions in any number of ways: as gut feelings or hunches; as "coincidentally" meeting a dietician or being drawn to a vegetarian book; as hearing an inner voice; or seeing visions about food.

The angels say that all food has internal messages and that these messages affect us, long after you have digested the food. As you attune your body to a higher and higher frequency, the angels will ask you to eat whole and natural foods.

Usually, the angels first ask you to eliminate red meats. Next, they request that you remove chicken and turkey, followed by fish. Animal flesh interferes with divine communication because it carries the energy of pain that the animal endured during its life and death. Pain energy has the lowest and densest vibration of all, and if you consume pain-filled food, your nervous system cannot reach its highest frequency potential.

Next, the angels will probably counsel that you cut back on stimulants such as caffeine, sugar, chocolate, and certain herbs. They may ask you to stop all stimulants completely, or they may guide you toward a gradual cessation. They will also eliminate other mood-altering chemicals, such as alcohol and nicotine.

Then, your angels may guide you to cut out some or all dairy products, as these foods can clog up our thinking and feeling channels. If this happens, you will either receive guidance that sends you to a good nutritionist or nutritional book, or the angels will ask you to eat vegan protein substitutes such as tofu or nuts.

As you purify your body more and more, you'll naturally gravitate toward a diet rich in fresh, organic produce, and baked goods made with sprouted grains. Your dietary changes won't feel like deprivation, but will, instead, feel rooted in love and joy. You'll easily adapt to each lifestyle change toward which the angels lovingly guide you. Each step of the way, you'll be aware that you ultimately have the final say-so about your diet.

Nevertheless, since you desire to hear the heavenly voice, you'll naturally choose to take all steps that clarify your channel of communication.

♥ ♥ ♥

Clearing Your Relationship with God

Sometimes people become estranged from God. Perhaps they suffered a huge disappointment and believe God let them down. Or they may have suffered pain at the hands of members of a religious group. Very often, estrangement from God stems from confusion about spirituality, religion, and the nature of God and man.

It's difficult to hear the voice of God and the angels when you feel distanced from heaven. However, since our higher self is eternally united with its Creator in heaven, we can't completely absolve ourselves of thoughts of God. Deep down, we long to enjoy the comfort of complete oneness with the angels and God.

Do you wonder sometimes if God loves other people more than you? Does it seem that others receive greater attention and rewards than you do? Did you suffer a loss that caused you to question God's motives? Were you raised to be afraid of God?

God and the angels know just how you feel. They know, because your feelings and thoughts are plainly visible in the spiritual world. All of your disappointments, hurts, and fears flash like giant neon signs around you.

The angels really want to help you regain the joy of loving God! They ask for your willingness to hand the entire situation over to them for repair. Tell God and the angels about all your cares, upsets, and fears. Don't worry—there are no repercussions for honesty, especially since they are already aware of everything you're going to say. Mainly, your heavenly supporters ask you to get your feelings off your chest.

After you've leveled with God and the angels about all of your frustrations, disappointments, and fears, they will ask if you'd like to exchange your painful thoughts for a more peaceful set of beliefs. If you agree, then, the angels will immediately set about to heal your relationship with God and heaven. Miraculously, you'll find that your thoughts and feelings shift to a new perspective.

This healing is on a very deep level. First, since your higher self is one with God, you'll find that your healed relationship with God extends to a better self-relationship. You'll feel happier about who you are, because you'll truly be loving your self as you love God. Second, since all the angels and earthly creatures are one with God, you'll feel greater compassion for, and a deeper connection with, others.

No matter what you need help with, no matter what you believe your blocks or limitations to be, the angels have a solution waiting for you right now. Just ask them.

♥ ♥ ♥

Spirit Releasement with Archangel Michael

Sensitive people—also known as clairsentients or empaths—frequently absorb others' energies. You may recall that a "clairsentient" is someone who is highly intuitive and who receives divine communication through physical sensations and emotional feelings.

Unwittingly, clairsentients take on another's fears and worries like a sponge drinks up water. This is especially true of clairsentient healers and teachers, whose caring nature attracts people to pour their troubles out to them. The troubled person feels relieved and unburdened after talking about her worries. However, the clairsentient feels drained or heavy because she has taken on the other person's troubles.

A burdened person is less able to help the world, so it is important for clairsentients to protect and clear their energy fields:

— *Avoid places where people abuse alcohol and other drugs.* These environments attract earthbound deceased people, who vicariously enjoy the companionship of intoxicated individuals. Sensitive lightworkers are prone to hitchhiking earthbound spirits, so it's best to avoid bars, cocktail parties, and discotheques.

— *Avoid places filled with ego-ridden mind-sets.* These include companies with manipulative philosophies, media sources that sell gossip and fear, organizations built upon competition or jealousy, and groups with low morale.

— *Shield yourself with light.* If you must enter these environments, protect yourself by visualizing a white wall of light, at least one inch thick, surrounding you like a shield. You can put one wall between yourself and the other person, or you can box yourself in completely.

— *Focus on love, light, and truth.* Whenever you talk to a person who is in an ego mind-set, continually claim the truth either mentally or aloud. Do not allow yourself to view the other person's fears as real, or you will invoke your own ego. Remember always that as you see others, so you see yourself. It's best to listen sympathetically as you would if these people were describing a scary movie that frightened them terribly. You would empathize with their feelings, while simultaneously knowing that the source of their fear was unreal.

♥ ♥ ♥

The Archangel Michael is the supreme protector and guardian angel of the Earth. He clears the planet and its population of darkness. If you feel drained or irritable, chances are that you have absorbed darkness. This darkness is nothing, in reality, because it is fear or the illusion of the absence of love. Since it is impossible that love is absent, there is nothing to fear. However, while we believe we live in bodies in a material planet, the earthbound rules affect us. One of those rules is that dark energy lowers our energy and mood.

The moment you become aware of feeling depleted or upset, you can be sure that an unloving thought is behind it. You have probably identified with someone else's fears or worries in some way, either because you judged them, felt sorry for them, or became angry with them. When we identify with others' fears *in any way*, we absorb their dark energy as we become one with them through our empathy.

In these times, you needn't struggle alone to rid yourself of darkness and absorbed fear. Instead, call upon the Archangel Michael. He doesn't need a formal invocation, just a sincere desire for his help. Saying or thinking, "Michael, please help me!" is enough to evoke his assistance instantly.

You'll know Michael is near because you'll feel a strong, sudden air pressure change. His presence feels like an etheric hug, reassuring yet not co-dependent. Michael loves us and protects us, but he does not view us as helpless—he sees our true power!

Then ask Michael (either mentally or aloud) to clear you of all darkness. You needn't help Michael in any way. In fact, when we try to help Michael help us, we often get in his way. It's best to just step back and become completely vulnerable and trusting of his help. Don't withhold any secrets or issues from Michael—he can see them all, anyway. Still, he cannot help you with areas that you withhold from his healing touch.

You might feel Michael opening the top of your head, the crown chakra area. Michael and his helpers, known as the "Band of Mercy," may enter your body and pick the dark thought-forms out of your cells as if they were picking apples. Michael also uses a tool similar to a vacuum to suction the darkness out of you very quickly. When the darkness is gone, he reverses the vacuum so that it pours a thick, toothpastelike white energy into your body to fill you where darkness previously resided.

You may also feel Michael cutting "etheric cords" that stretch between you and another person. Everyone—not just clairsentients—builds these cords with people to whom we are close. They look like arteries and they come in varying degrees of thickness. Usually, etheric cords are attached to our major chakra energy centers, such as heart-to-heart, or solar plexus-to-solar plexus. These cords don't pose a problem when they connect two highly evolved people. However, you may have a cord attached to, for example, a sibling who is enduring life crises. In such cases, your sibling is likely feeding off your energy through your attached etheric cord. So you will feel drained without knowing why. The reason is that your sibling is acting as an energy robber, instead of tapping into her own natural source of energy.

When you call Archangel Michael to help you revive your energy and outlook, he uses his sword to cut away etheric cords that drain you. Michael and his Band of Mercy (his angelic assistants) also gather up stray earthbound spirits attached to you. These earthbound people belong in the afterlife plane. Michael escorts them to the light for their own spiritual growth. Very often, earthbound people do not realize they are dead. In other cases, earthbounds are afraid of going to the light. Sometimes they fear a punishing, angry God. Other times, they don't want to leave the material possessions accumulated during their earthly life. As mentioned earlier, some earthbounds who abused alcohol and drugs during their lifetime hang around bars and parties to absorb the energy of intoxication.

Empathetic lightworkers must vigilantly monitor their energy and mood levels to ensure against a build-up of psychic dirt from fears, worries, and earthbound spirits. Never fear that you are wearing out your welcome with Archangel Michael. He can be in many places and with many people simultaneously because he lives in a dimension unfettered by time or space beliefs. You can ask him to live with you if you like. There are no restrictions or limitations, except those you decide for yourself.

Of course, having Michael next to our side does not allow us to disobey our inner Voice of God, which gives us rational guidance about staying safe in the material earthplane. If your inner teacher warns you to stay away from a certain locale, it would not be wise to ignore this warning just because you have asked Michael to accompany you. Michael is a wonderful server and protector, but he—like God and all the angels—will not usurp our personal responsibility for making decisions.

♥ ♥ ♥

Spiritual Safety

You are safe in this world, in truth, for nothing can harm who you really are. Death, injury, and loss are illusions of the material world. Holding these truths in your heart and mind is your ultimate secret that allows you to walk in complete safety, wherever you are.

The angels will help you to feel safe and protected by surrounding you with their loving energy. For example, before you go to sleep at night, visualize your home surrounded by white light. This is a very real way to "seal" your home and insulate it against any lower-thought energies. Then, mentally ask for four guardian angels to stand post at the north, south, east, and westerly sides of your home.

Let's say that a person is ridden with ego thoughts such as, "I must steal from others to meet my material needs." Let's also suppose that this person is roaming your neighborhood at night, believing that robbery is their source of income. Your home, protected by angels, will repel this ego-bound person. He will not know *why*, but your home will not attract him.

Penetrating the loving guardianship of angels is impossible for any negative forces. The angelic energy deflects the lower-self energy of those with unholy intentions, like two magnets pushing each other away. The angels will also warn you, should you need information to avoid a dangerous situation. This is another reason why it's a good idea to go to bed with a clear and sober mind. After all, we need to have access to our dreams for our growth, safety, and protection.

Ask your angels to surround you and your loved ones always. When I'm on airplanes, I ask angels to surround and support the aircraft. In cars, I call upon angels to guide the vehicle and protect its tires, chassis, and engine.

If you are in an unfamiliar environment, or anywhere that you feel unsafe or dishonored, call upon the angels for protection. Walking down a lonely street, your angels will fly ahead of you and clear your path. In a situation where someone has unkind or dishonest intentions, your angels will intervene for you. If someone is about to betray you, you'll receive warnings from your angels as strong gut feelings. Please don't ignore these invisible answers to your prayers!

Instead of trying to control or fix negative situations on a human level, your angels will work with you from the spiritual plane. They will continuously remind you that you have all the power you need, right inside yourself. You and the angels are kin, in that you both are creations of the same all-powerful, all-loving Maker. You can call upon your divine power to heal any situation, and team up with your angels to shine truth and love wherever you go.

Our loved ones are so important, and you can send angels to guide, guard, and protect them. Visualize your child surrounded by dozens of wise and loving angels. Know that your visualization is the invitation that instantly brings angelic beings to your child's side. If you have a friend in distress, ask angels to comfort and help her.

You also help to guide and guard your city, nation, and planet by sending angels to political and military power centers. Pray that The Angelic Realm surrounds government leaders with higher wisdom and heavenly love. See angels happily hovering about the capitols and courthouses of the world. Know that your visualizations contribute powerful healing energy that attunes leaders' minds to the highest good for all concerned. The angels help these leaders lose their lower-self ego concerns, and connect with the one universal mind of divine intelligence.

❤ ❤ ❤

Angel Therapy

I've been a spiritual psychologist for many years and have seen or tried nearly every form of therapy available. I hold B.A., M.A., and Ph.D. degrees in psychology and have been director of two inpatient and three outpatient psychiatric programs. I've stood beside psychiatrists who administered electro-shock therapy, various drugs, and traditional psychoanalysis. I've witnessed Jungian, Freudian, and Rogerian therapy at work. I've attended workshops given by psychological greats such as Carl Rogers, Rollo May, and William Glasser. I mention all this as a basis for what I'm about to share.

While working with clients who have long-standing emotional blocks—usually, old resentments held toward themselves, an abuser, parent, sibling, or ex-spouse—I've discovered that the only barrier in their way is their *decision to release these blocks.* If a person decides to stay unhappy, no amount of therapy is going to be effective. It is only when the person says, "I am *willing* to be healed," that healing occurs.

Very often, clients are unwilling to heal because they fear repercussions related to their emotional and physical health. They fear boredom from a life that is crisis-free. They fear making changes in their thoughts and behaviors. They fear that health, or the process of getting healthy, would be more painful than illness.

That is where angel therapy comes in. Angel therapy is the fastest, most effective, and most enjoyable form of healing I have ever found. I have the angels to thank for introducing me to their therapeutic methods. Following the angel's warning about my car being stolen, I began asking my angels for advice in all areas of my life—including my counseling work.

Their advice about healing continued throughout the writing of this book. The messages I received in Part I have influenced my current counseling work. They taught me the method described in this chapter and assured me that it would be well received. I initially used it with my long-term clients, who expressed great satisfaction with the angel therapy. Then, I began teaching and demonstrating this method with my seminar audiences. After I consistently received positive feedback about angel therapy's results, I decided to incorporate it into all of my sessions.

Today, my work consists of listening to and relaying to my clients, the messages I hear from their angels. I use a combination of clairvoyance, clairaudience, and angel oracle cards to receive these angel messages. After we identify emotional blocks that are challenging my client, we use angel therapy to clear the blocks away. Common blocks that the angels identify in our sessions include low self-esteem, money obsessions, unforgiveness toward self or another, jealousy, feeling unsafe, and a fear of not fulfilling one's life purpose.

Angel therapy starts with the understanding that whenever you feel pain—emotional or physical—it means you have chosen a thought from your lower-self, or ego. I'll give you a brief summary of how this occurs. The details about the ego aren't crucial for angel therapy to work; however, understanding the dynamics of pain and of healing is helpful.

Since God only created love, pain is unreal. Pain is rooted in ego-based thoughts of, "I am separate from God and other people." The ego is completely incapable of love, and it creates thoughts ranging from irritation to murder. Sometimes, spiritual seekers are horrified that they have violent and unloving thoughts. They think, *Something's wrong with me! A spiritual person shouldn't think this way,* and they conclude that they've backslid upon the spiritual path.

When we judge an ego thought as "bad" or "wrong," though, we give the ego power and the illusion of reality. A better way to handle ego thoughts is based upon the Eastern approach: Simply notice it without judgment. Say to yourself, "Oh, I see that I'm having an ego thought of anger, jealousy, competition, or (fill in the blank)."

All thoughts create etheric forms, which clairvoyantly look like soap bubbles. There are no neutral thoughts or periods of time when your thoughts don't create a form. These forms go out in the physical world and manifest into creations that mirror your thoughts.

In angel therapy, you notice your ego thought and then call upon angels to surround and encircle you. Instantly, they will be by your side. Perhaps you can see them or feel their presence by an air-pressure change around you.

Picture or feel your ego thought as a soap bubble about the size of a clear cantaloupe. Mentally image yourself holding the thought-form in the hand with which you normally write. This is your releasing hand. Then, see or feel yourself handing this thought-form bubble to the angels.

They immediately take your thought-form away, to the Light, where they purify it. The angels return your thought-form to you in its purist form, which is love. This love may contain ideas that will help you transform some personality trait or circumstance in your life. In this way, you can correct whatever habits created the original ego thought initially.

After you feel the release from pain, it's important to thank your angels. Your gratitude and happiness is their "paycheck" for services rendered. If you'll join them in giving glory to God—Who is one with your higher self—the angels are doubly delighted.

♥ ♥ ♥

Enfolded in Angel Wings

You are never alone, and angels accompany you constantly, even when you are unaware of their presence. The angels want to interact with you more frequently. They'd love to be fully involved with every aspect of your life, yet they cannot help you unless you specifically ask. Like many practices that are good for us, such as meditation and exercise, we benefit by making angel communication a regular part of our life. Surround yourself with reminders, such as angel statues and posters, so you won't forget to call upon your heavenly friends for help and assistance.

We needn't wait until crisis or pressure has hit before asking our angels for help. In fact, it's a good idea to work with your angels in any trying situation before it gets to the boiling point. However, if you forget to include your angels in your plans, they still will answer your call of "Help" if you get into a jam.

There are no limits to what your angels can do in your life. They are very, very powerful beings. Once you invite them into your life, get ready, because your life *will* change in very miraculous ways. If you don't quite yet fully believe in angels, you will know that they are real after asking for and receiving their help two or three times.

The Angelic Realm loves you, and they see you as you truly are on the inside—as an innocent and perfect child of God. They know that you have made occasional mistakes just like the rest of us. Yet, angels overlook our errors and see the love and good intentions within our hearts. See yourself and others through the eyes of an angel, and you'll see a beautiful world that is light, bright, and hopeful.

You *are* an angel, and you are a blessing to the world.

SELF-HELP RESOURCES

The following list of resources can be used to access information on a variety of issues. The addresses, telephone numbers and websites listed below are usually for the national headquarters; look in your local Yellow Pages under "Community Services" for resources closer to your area. In addition to the following groups, other self-help organizations may be available in your area to assist your healing and recovery for a particular life crisis not listed here. Consult your telephone directory, call a counseling centre or helpline near you, or contact the following organizations.

AIDS

National AIDS Helpline
Tel: 0845 122 1200

Terrence Higgins Trust
Tel: 020 7242 1010
Tel: 0845 1221 200
www.info@tht.org.uk

Positively Women
347-349 City Road
London EC1V 1LR
Tel: 020 7713 0222/0444

ALCOHOL ABUSE

Alcoholics Anonymous
PO Box 1 Stonebow House
Stonebow York YO1 7NJ
Tel: 01904 644026
www.alcoholics-anony-mous.org.uk

Al-Anon Family Groups
61 Great Dover Street
London SE1 4YF
Tel: 020 7403 0888
www.al-anonuk.org.uk

National Association for Children of Alcoholics
PO Box 64 Fishponds
Bristol BS16 2UH
Tel: 0800 358 3456
www.nacoa.org.uk

Alcohol Concern
Waterbridge House
32-36 Loman Street
London SE1 0EE
Tel: 020 7928 7377

Children and Family Alcohol and Drugs Service CAFADS

Unit 202 Bow House
153-159 Bow House
London E3 2SE
Tel: 020 8983 4861
www.cafads.org.uk

ALZHEIMER'S DISEASE

Alzheimer's Society
Gordon House
10 Greencoat Place
London SW1P 1PH
Tel: 020 7306 0606
www.alz.co.uk

Care Aware (Elderly Care Funding Advice)
PO Box 8
Manchester M30 9NY
Tel: 0870 513 4925
www.careaware.co.uk

CANCER

Cancer BACUP Helpline
Tel: 0808 800 1234
Tel: 0845 634 1414
18 and under:
Tel: 0845 347 650 or
text: 0797 749 3345

National Cancer Research Institute
PO Box 123
61 Lincoln's Inn Fields
London WC2A 3PX
Tel: 020 7061 8460
www.ncri.org.uk

CHILDREN'S ISSUES

Child Molestation

www.childline.org.uk
Tel: 0800 1111

National Association for People Abused in Childhood (NAPAC)
42 Curtain Road
London EC2A 3NH
www.napac.org.uk

National Society for the Prevention of Cruelty to Children (NSPCC)
Weston House 42 Curtain
Road London EC2A 3NH
Tel: 020 7825 2500
www.nspcc.org.uk

Crisis Intervention

CRISIS (Helping Young People Overcome Addictions and Mental Health Problems)
666 Commercial Street
London E1 6LT
Tel: 0870 011 3335
www.crisis.org

Shelter
88 Old Street
London EC1V 9HU
Tel: 0845 458 4590
www.england.shelter.org.uk

Runaway Helpline
Tel: 0808 800 7070

Message Home Helpline (For People Who Want to Send a Message Home without Being Contacted Themselves)
Tel: 0800 700 740

Missing Children

National Missing Person's Helpline
Tel: 0500 700 700
uk.missingkids.com
Children with Serious Illnesses (fulfilling wishes)

Children's Wish
24 Welbeck Way
London W1G 9YR
Tel: 020 7034 1910
www.childrenswish.co.uk

Starlight Children's Foundation
Room PRW1
Macmillan House
Paddington Station
London W2 1HD
Tel: 020 7262 2881
www.starlight.org.uk

DEATH/GRIEVING/ SUICIDE

CRUSE (Bereavement Care)
Cruse House
126 Sheen Road
Richmond
Surrey TW9 1UR
Tel: 0870 167 1677
www.crusebereavement-care.org.uk

Child Death Helpline
Great Ormond
St Hospital for Children
London WC1N 2AP
Tel: 0800 282 986
www.childdeathhelpline.org.uk

Samaritans (Suicide Helpline)
Tel: 0845 790 9090
www.samaritans.org.uk
www.jo@samaritans.org

DEBTS

Consumer Credit Counselling Service
Wode House Merrion Centre
Leeds LS2 8NG
Tel: 0800 138 1111
www.cccs.co.uk

Debtors Anonymous
Tel: 020 7644 5070
www.debtorsanonymous.info

DIABETES

Diabetes UK
10 Parkway
London NW1 7AA
Tel: 020 7424 1000
www.diabetes.org.uk

DOMESTIC VIOLENCE

Domestic Violence Helpline
Tel: 0808 200 0247

DRUG ABUSE

Cocaine Anonymous
www.ca.org.uk

Narcotics Anonymous
202 City Road
London EC1V 2PH
Tel: 020 7730 0009
www.ukna.org

National Drugs Helpline
Tel: 0800 587 5879
www.knowthescore.info
www.addaction.org.uk

Release
388 Old Street
London EC1V 9LT
www.release.org.uk

EATING DISORDERS

Overeaters Anonymous
PO Box 19
Stretford
Manchester M32 9EB
Tel: 0700 0784 985
www.oagb.org.uk

GAMBLING

Gamblers Anonymous
PO Box 88
London SW10 0EU
Tel: 0870 050 88 80
www.gamblersanonymous.org.uk

HEALTH

Pain Relief Foundation
Clinical Sciences Centre
University Hospital
Aintree Lower Lane
Liverpool L9 7AL
Tel: 0151 529 5820
www.painrelieffoundation.org.uk

Institute for Complementary Medicine
PO Box 194
London SE16 1QZ
Tel: 020 7237 5165
www.i-c-m.org.uk

Federation of Holistic Therapists
3rd Floor, Eastleigh House
Upper Market Street
Eastleigh Hants SO50 9FD
Tel: 0870 420 2022
www.fht.org.uk

Koestler Parapsychology Unit
PPLS
University of Edinburgh
7 George Square
Edinburgh EH8 9LZ
Tel: 0131 650 3348

National Institute of Medical Herbalists
Elm House
54 Mary Arches Street
Exeter EX4 3BA
Tel: 01392 426 022

Natural Health Advisory Service
PO Box 268
Lewes East
Sussex BN7 1QN
Tel: 0906 255 6615
www.naturalhealthas.com

Mind Body Spirit Directory
www.BodyMindSpiritDIRECTORY.org

National Council for Hypnotherapy
www.hypnotherapists.org.uk

HOUSING RESOURCES

Shelter
88 Old Street
London EC1V 9HU
Tel: 0845 458 4590
www.england.shelter.org.
uk

Housing Associations
www.direct.gov.uk

IMPOTENCE

The Sexual Dysfunction Association
Tel: 0870 774 3571

MENTAL HEALTH

MIND
15-19 Broadway
London E15 4BQ
Tel: 0845 766 0163
www.mind.org.uk

National Institute for Mental Health
NIMHE Central Room
8E46, Quarry House
Quarry Hill
Leeds LS2 7UE
Tel: 0113 254 5127
www.nimhe.org.uk

SANE
1st Floor, Cityside House
40 Adler Street
London E1 1EE
Tel: 0845 767 8000
www.sane.org.uk

UK Trauma Group (for Post-Traumatic Stress)
www.uktrauma.org.uk

Depression Alliance
35 Westminster Bridge
Road London SE1 7JB
Tel: 0845 123 2320
www.depressionalliance.
org

PET BEREAVEMENT

Pet Bereavement Support Service

Tel: 0800 096 6606
www.bluecross.org.uk

RAPE/SEXUAL ISSUES

Rape and Sexual Abuse Counselling Service (RASAC)
Women's Helpline:
Tel: 01962 848024
Men's Helpline:
Tel: 01962 848027
www.rasac.org.uk

Sexaholics Anonymous
Tel: 0700 0725 463
www.sauk.org

Playing Safely (Advice on Sexually Transmitted Diseases)
Tel: 0800 567 123
www.playingsafely.co.uk

SMOKING

QUIT
Tel: 0800 002200
www.quit.org.uk

ASH (Action on Smoking and Health)
www.ash.org.uk

STRESS REDUCTION

Association for Applied Psychophysiology and Biofeedback
www.aapb.org

Resurgence (Magazine of the Omega Institute)
Ford House
Hartland Bideford
Devon EX39 6EE
Tel: 01237 441 293
www.resurgence.org

TEEN HELP

The Site
YouthNet UK
3rd Floor 2-3 Upper Street
London N1 0PQ
Tel: 020 7226 8008
www.thesite.org

Centrepoint (Supporting Homeless Young People)

Neil House
7 Whitechapel Road
London E1 1DU
Tel: 020 7426 5300

Eating Disorders Association
103 Prince of Wales Road
Norwich NR1 1DW
Tel: 0845 347 650 or
text: 0797 749 3345
www.edauk.com

Family Planning Association 2-12
Pentonville Road
London N1 9FP
Tel: 0845 310 1334
www.fpa.org.uk

Papyrus (Charity committed to Suicide Prevention, especially for Teenagers and Young Adults)
Rossendale GH Union
Road Rawtenstall
Lancashire BB4 6NE
Tel: 01706 214 449
www.papyrus-uk.org

Helplines for Teenagers

Childline
Tel: 0800 849 4545

Teenage Pregnancy
Tel: 0800 849 4545
www.preghelp.org.uk

Runaway Helpline
Tel: 0808 800 7070

Message Home Helpline (for People Who Want to Send a Message Home without Being Contacted Themselves)
Tel: 0800 700 740

♥ ♥ ♥

About Doreen Virtue, Ph.D.

As the daughter of a spiritual healer, Doreen Virtue grew up with miraculous experiences. However, nothing prepared her for the angelic intervention that saved her life during a carjacking episode. Her brush with death caused Doreen to ask the angels for answers, guidance, and help. The angels answered her request with clear, loving, and beautiful words. Doreen holds Ph.D., M.A., and B.A. degrees in counseling psychology; and she is the former director of two inpatient psychiatric hospital units. After she began working with The Angelic Realm, Doreen taught her clients and workshop audiences how to hear the voices of their own guardian angels. In *Angel Therapy,* she brings the heavenly messages to readers.

Doreen is a spiritual doctor of psychology who teaches her clients how to heal the emotions, mind, and body with angelic intervention – what she terms "Angel Therapy." Doreen gives workshops across the country about ways to hear Divine Guidance. To receive her workshop schedule, please call or write to Hay House.

If you would like to contact Doreen Virtue,
please write to her in care of Hay House or you may
visit her Website: **www.AngelTherapy.com**

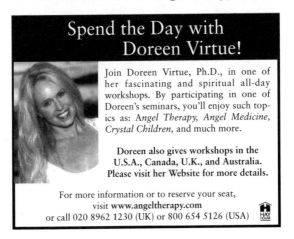

We hope you enjoyed this Hay House book.
If you would like to receive a free catalogue featuring additional
Hay House books and products, or if you would like information
about the Hay Foundation, please contact:

Hay House UK Ltd
292B Kensal Road • London W10 5BE
Tel: (44) 20 8962 1230; Fax: (44) 20 8962 1239
www.hayhouse.co.uk

****

Published and distributed in the United States of America by:
Hay House, Inc. • P.O. Box 5100 • Carlsbad, CA 92018-5100
Tel: (1) 760 431 7695 or (800) 654 5126;
Fax: (1) 760 431 6948 or (800) 650 5115
www.hayhouse.com

****

Published and distributed in Australia by:
Hay House Australia Ltd • 18/36 Ralph St • Alexandria NSW 2015
Tel: (61) 2 9669 4299 • Fax: (61) 2 9669 4144
www.hayhouse.com.au

****

Published and distributed in the Republic of South Africa by:
Hay House SA (Pty) Ltd • PO Box 990 • Witkoppen 2068
Tel/Fax: (27) 11 467 8904 • www.hayhouse.co.za

****

Distributed in Canada by:
Raincoast • 9050 Shaughnessy St • Vancouver, BC V6P 6E5
Tel: (1) 604 323 7100 • Fax: (1) 604 323 2600

****

Sign up via the Hay House UK website to receive the Hay House
online newsletter and stay informed about what's going on with
your favourite authors. You'll receive bimonthly announcements
about discounts and offers, special events, product highlights,
free excerpts, giveaways, and more!
www.hayhouse.co.uk